Hors d'Oeuvres & Appetizers

Hors d'Oeuvres & Appetizers

Elizabeth Price

Editor: **Margo Coughtrie**
Assistant Editor: **Sally Fisher**
Designers: **Roger Hammond**
Jan Churcher

CHARTWELL BOOKS INC.

in association with Phoebus

Mushroom and Cheese Vol-au-Vents.

Contents

The cover picture shows: background from right to left, Tomatoes Bonne Femme, Kippered Herrings Vinaigrette, Crab Dip with parsley, Avocado and Walnut Dip and Savory Shrimp Tartlets.

Published by Chartwell Books Inc.
A Division of Book Sales Inc.
110 Enterprise Avenue
Secaucus, New Jersey 07094

Library of Congress Catalog Card
Number: 77–74635

This edition © 1978 Phoebus
Publishing Company/BPC Publishing Limited,
169 Wardour Street, London W1A 2JX

Made and printed in Great Britain by Waterlow (Dunstable) Limited

ISBN 0–89009–128–5

Deep Fried Sardines.

Introduction

Few aspects of entertaining offer such a challenge to the imaginative cook as the preparation of hors d'oeuvres and appetizers. Collected together in this book you will find a host of ideas for party savories, cocktail canapés, appetizers and salads suitable for almost every occasion. So, whether you are planning a formal dinner party, a family supper or an informal cocktail party, this book will provide all the answers.

We devote a chapter to canapés and hors d'oeuvres, which are ideal to serve with drinks before dinner or at a buffet or cocktail party.

We give a wide choice of appetizers, hot and cold, suitable for summer or winter, with serving ideas and suggestions for garnishing. There is another chapter on pâtés, ranging from the simple to the more sophisticated.

To help you become the perfect hostess, Hors d'Oeuvres and Appetizers is fully illustrated. There are helpful step-by-step photographs and all the sauces, dressings and garnishes you need to give your entertaining that special touch.

Scrambled Eggs with Shrimps.

Canapés and hors d'oeuvres

Canapés and hors d'oeuvres add the final touch to parties both formal and informal. It is important to provide a variety of color, texture and flavor whether you are serving simple dips or more elaborate hors d'oeuvres. To combine well with the drinks you are serving, choose fairly pronounced flavors such as cheese, anchovy and caviare.

Don't tackle too many types at once. 8–10 different kinds should be enough for a group of 50, and 4–5 kinds for up to 24 people. For formal gatherings allow 6 hors d'oeuvres or canapés per guest, and slightly more for informal parties.

Prepare everything well in advance so that they only need to be assembled and arranged on trays and platters before serving. Use plenty of color for garnishing, such as parsley, watercress, tomatoes and lemons.

Prepared trays of chilled hors d'oeuvres and canapés can be kept fresh with damp towels or plastic wrap. Food to be reheated can be ready on cookie sheets.

Finally, to keep your guests well supplied, have some in reserve to replenish the dishes during the party.

Flaky Cheese Puffs served hot with a sprinkling of paprika.

Flaky Cheese Puffs

basic puff pastry made from 1 cup flour
¾ lb Gruyère or Emmentaler cheese
1 egg
a little prepared English mustard
salt and pepper

Set the oven at 375°F.

Make up the pastry, if not already in freezer. Cut cheese into slices, about 4 inches long, 1 inch wide, and ½ inch thick. Lightly beat the egg.

Roll out pastry thinly and cut into rectangles, each about 1 inch longer than the cheese slices and wide enough to wrap around them. Spread a little mustard over each piece of pastry, moisten edges and place a slice of cheese on each. Roll up pastry and seal the edges. Place on a cookie sheet lined with nonstick silicone or waxed paper and brush the top of each with a little beaten egg.

Bake in the preset oven until golden brown and cooked. Serve hot.

You can make these in advance and chill in the refrigerator. Bake as required.

Flaky Fish Puffs

basic puff pastry made from 1½ cups flour
6 small kippered herring fillets
1 egg
pepper

Set the oven at 400°F.

Make up pastry. Cut each fillet in half. Lightly beat the egg.

Roll out pastry very thinly and cut into rectangles, each large enough to wrap around a halved kippered herring fillet. Moisten pastry edges, place a halved fillet on each and roll up, sealing edges. Place each puff, with the pastry joins underneath, on a cookie sheet lined with nonstick silicone paper. Brush the top of each with beaten egg and season, if liked, with a sprinkling of pepper.

Bake in the preset oven for 15–20 minutes. Serve hot.

Canapés and hors d'oeuvres

Classic Chicken Slice

basic savory shortcrust pastry made from
1½ cups flour
¼–⅓ cup cooked chicken or veal – or a
mixture of both
about ¼ cup mushrooms, finely chopped
2 tbsp butter
2 tbsp flour
1 cup chicken stock
¼–⅜ cup light cream
1 tbsp chopped parsley (optional)
1 egg
salt and pepper

Set the oven at 375°F.

Make up pastry and chill. Cut the cooked meat into dice. Beat the egg.

Melt the butter in a pan over low heat, stir in flour and blend until a smooth straw colored roux is obtained. Add chicken stock, little by little, stirring well all the time. Add mushrooms, diced meat, cream and, if liked, a tablespoon of chopped parsley. Adjust seasoning. (The sauce should be thick enough to lightly coat the meat).

Roll out the pastry into a rectangle about 12 inches long and 4–5 inches wide. Decorate by snipping v-shapes down each long side. Spoon meat mixture along the center, moisten pastry edges and fold long sides up to the center. Press well together, otherwise the pastry will fall back during cooking and expose filling. Seal and tuck ends under. Brush with beaten egg and bake in the preset oven for about 25–30 minutes, or until golden brown and cooked. Serve hot or cold, cut into fingers.

To make the filling go further, or to replace some of the meat, add a couple of chopped hardcooked eggs.

Serve Classic Chicken Slice, Fish Finger Pies and Curry Morsels for informal parties.

Fish Finger Pies

basic savory puff pastry made from 1 cup
flour
1 fillet cooked white fish
(cod or haddock)
⅔ cup basic white sauce
1 hardcooked egg
a few drops anchovy flavoring
a little beaten egg

Set the oven at 375°F.

Make up pastry, if not in freezer. Flake fish, peel and chop egg. Prepare sauce.

Roll out pastry very thinly and line into finger-shaped patty pans (or tartlet pans if you have no finger-shaped pans). Reroll trimmings and cut out lids, using a pastry base as a guide. Place fish and sauce in a basin and beat to mix. Add anchovy flavoring and mix again before adding egg. Spoon a little of the mixture into each pastry base, moisten edges with beaten egg and cover with a pastry lid. Glaze with beaten egg.

Bake in the preset oven for 12 minutes, or until golden brown and cooked.

Curry Morsels

savory shortcrust pastry made from 1 cup
    flour
scant ½ cup ground, cooked meat (lamb,
    pork, or beef)
1 shallot or small onion
2 tbsp shortening or oil for frying
1 tbsp flour
⅔ cup stock or water
¼ tsp garam masala, or curry paste
a little beaten egg
salt and pepper

Set the oven at 375°F.

Peel and finely chop shallot or onion.
Grease and flour 9–12 tiny 'petit four'
pans approximately 1½ inches in diameter
and ½ inch deep.
   Melt shortening in a pan over low heat,
add shallot or onion and sauté until transparent. Sprinkle flour over and blend in to
thicken, then add garam masala or curry
paste and, little by little, the stock or
water. Stir until sauce is smooth. Add
ground meat and season to taste. Leave to
cool slightly.
   Roll out pastry very thinly and cut into
rounds to line the tiny pans. Cut out lids of
appropriate diameter. Place a little filling
in each base, moisten pastry edges and
cover with pastry lid. Place each on a
cookie sheet, if the molds are not in one
'tray', and lightly brush lids with beaten
egg (add a pinch of salt to liquify the egg
and make a shinier glaze).
   Bake in the preset oven for 10 minutes,
or until pastry is brown and crisp. Serve
hot.

Garam Masala

Garam masala can be bought from shops
specializing in Indian food, but it will have
a fresher flavor if you make your own.

3 tsp cinnamon
1 tsp ground cloves
3 tsp cardamom seeds
1 tsp black cumin seeds
good pinch mace
good pinch ground nutmeg

Pound or grind ingredients together and
store in an airtight container. It will keep
almost indefinitely, but it does tend to lose
its strength eventually.

HOW TO MAKE BASIC PUFF PASTRY

4 cups flour
pinch salt
2 cups butter
2 tsp lemon juice
scant 1 cup ice cold water

1. Sift flour and salt onto a cold surface.
Dice ¾ cup of butter and rub in gently.

2. When flour is rubbed in and resembles
fine breadcrumbs, shape into a mound.

3. Mix lemon juice and water and using 2
knives gradually work the liquid into the
mixture until a smooth dough is formed.

4. Work the dough into a smooth ball with
your hands. Sift a little flour over the
dough, fold it in a clean cloth and leave
refrigerator to rest.

5. Take the remaining butter from the
refrigerator and pat into a rectangle. Take
dough from refrigerator, roll out into a
rectangle and place butter in center.

6. Wrap dough around butter to form a
parcel. Turn 90°, roll out into a strip. Fold,
roll again. Refrigerate for 15 minutes.
Roll, fold, turn and refrigerate five times
in all before the pastry is ready to use.

HOW TO MAKE VOL-AU-VENT CASES AND BOUCHÉES

Make up basic puff pastry using 4 cups of flour.

Set the oven at 425°F.

1. Roll out rectangle ¾ inch thick. Cut bases with a 3 inch diameter cookie cutter and put on cookie sheet.

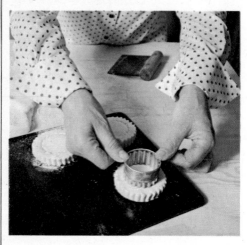

2. With a 2 inch diameter cookie cutter, cut through each round until three-quarters through. Brush with beaten egg and bake in preset oven for 15–20 minutes.

3. When cooked to a golden brown and cooled, remove top neatly with a teaspoon, leaving a cavity to be filled with the chosen filling.

Savory Vol-au-Vents with Kidney and Mushroom filling.

To Make Bouchées

Use exactly the same method as for vol-au-vent cases, but this time using really small cookie cutters, 1¾ inch and 1 inch in diameter. (If you cannot find a tiny 1 inch cookie cutter, try cutting out the lid shape with a sharp knife. Be careful not to cut through the base of the pastry.)

Fillings for Vol-au-Vents or Bouchées

Kidney and Mushroom

4 lambs' kidneys
2 cups button mushrooms
2 tbsp butter
¼ cup flour
1–2 tbsp dry sherry
⅔ cup stock
about ½ cup heavy cream
salt and pepper

Skin and blanch kidneys and leave in pan of hot water for 15 minutes. Wash and finely slice mushrooms.

Melt butter in a pan over gentle heat, remove kidneys from pan, pat dry with absorbent paper and slice finely. Sauté in the butter for 2–3 minutes, then add flour and stir until blended. Add sherry and, gradually, the stock, stirring all the time. Finally add mushrooms and stir in the cream.

Taste for seasoning and continue to simmer gently for 3–4 minutes over gentle heat. Do not allow kidneys to overcook.

Fill vol-au-vent cases with mixture, replace tops and heat through in the oven for a few minutes. Serve hot.

Chicken and Mushroom

½ cup cooked chicken
½ cup button mushrooms
1 tbsp flour
1 tbsp butter
⅜ cup dry white wine
⅛–¼ cup milk
⅜ cup light cream
salt and pepper

For garnish
1 cooked carrot
1 tbsp cooked peas
1 tbsp cooked green beans
1 or 2 stuffed green olives
a little basic aspic

Chop chicken meat, finely dice mushrooms, shred carrot, dice green beans, slice olives and prepare aspic.

Melt butter in a pan and, when melted, add flour. Stir to a straw colored roux, (this should take about 1 minute) then add white wine. Blend well, stirring vigorously, then add milk and bring to the boil. Using a balloon (wire) whisk, whisk up sauce until smooth, then add cream and continue whisking. Add mushrooms, cook for a few minutes before adding chicken and seasoning to taste.

Allow to cool before filling the cases and garnishing each with a sprinkling of diced vegetables, topped with a slice of stuffed olive. The topping can be kept in place with a touch of cool, jelling aspic. Otherwise, replace lid as usual and omit the garnish.

Creamed Pâté

2–3 oz pâté (homemade or bought)
1–2 tbsp light cream
dry sherry or brandy

Whip cream and add 1–2 tsp sherry or brandy, or to taste. Blend thoroughly with the pâté until smooth.

Seafood

1 cup prawns or shrimps
1 tbsp flour
1 tbsp butter
⅜ cup dry white wine
⅛–¼ cup milk
⅜ cup light cream
salt and pepper

For garnish
parsley, watercress

Make the sauce as for the Chicken and Mushroom filling. Add the prawns or shrimps and season to taste.

Allow to cool before filling the cases and garnish.

Stuffed Tomatoes in Almond Cups.

Savory Shortcrust Pastry

4 cups flour
1 tsp salt
¼ cup butter or margarine
¼ cup lard
¾ cup grated Cheddar or
*   Parmesan cheese*
1 egg yolk
6–8 tbsp cold water

Sift the flour and salt into a large mixing bowl. Cut the butter or margarine and lard into small pieces and put into the bowl. Work into the flour with the fingertips or a pastry blender until the mixture resembles fine breadcrumbs.

Stir in the grated cheese. Add the egg and a little water and stir to combine. Add more water gradually and stir until the dough begins to hold together.

Form dough into a ball with the fingers, turn out onto a floured board and knead lightly until smooth and free from cracks.

Wrap dough in foil and chill in the refrigerator for at least 1 hour before using.

Stuffed Tomatoes in Almond Cups

about 10 very small tomatoes

For savory paste
¾ cup finely ground almonds
¼ cup grated Parmesan cheese
1 egg white
salt and pepper

For cream cheese filling
3 oz package cream cheese
¼ cup heavy cream
dry sherry to taste
pinch of celery salt
pinch of cayenne pepper
salt and pepper

To make the almond cups, first place almonds and grated Parmesan in a bowl and lightly season. Mix together and gradually add the egg white, working the mixture to a paste with the fingertips or a wooden spoon. Roll out paste thinly and cut into small rounds about 3 inches in diameter or to fit the size of the tomatoes. Fill into individual dariole molds and shape into cups. Chill to set.

For the filling, lightly whip the cream and beat it into the cheese. Add sherry to taste, season with salt, pepper and celery salt and mix thoroughly.

Slice off tops of tomatoes and scoop out the seeds. Place a tsp of filling in each and sprinkle with cayenne pepper. Remove the almond cups from the molds using a knife and trim the tops into points all round with scissors. Arrange them on a serving dish and place a stuffed tomato in each.

Savory Tartlets

For party canapés, make pastry cases of basic shortcrust, lined into tiny greased and floured patty pans or bouchée cups, which are about 1¼–1½ inches in diameter and ½ inch deep. Only small quantities of filling will be required. Here are some suggestions.

Shrimp Mayonnaise

2 tbsp peeled and veined shrimps
2 tbsp heavy cream
2 tbsp basic mayonnaise

Chop the shrimps. Whip the cream until very thick. Bake the pastry cases blind in a hot oven at 400°F for a few minutes.

Fold shrimps into the cream and add the mayonnaise. Fill the cooled tartlets. To garnish, pipe a little cream cheese with a little extra cream to achieve the correct piping consistency around the tartlet and top with a toasted almond flake. Another variation is to garnish with a sprinkling of paprika and top with parsley.

Crab, Salmon or Lobster Mayonnaise

For 12 tartlets
2 tbsp crabmeat, cooked salmon
*   or lobster claw meat*
2 tbsp heavy cream
2 tbsp basic mayonnaise

Follow the method for Shrimp Mayonnaise. To garnish, make a shallow cut on the top. Sprinkle one half with paprika, the other with freshly ground black pepper or chopped pistachio nuts.

Savory Tartlets with some filling suggestions.

Savory Egg Turnovers are perfect when something more substantial is needed.

Heart-shaped Tartlets Niçoise.

Savory Egg Turnovers

7 eggs
basic puff pastry made from 2 cups flour
½ lb lean pork, finely ground
4 tbsp light cream

Set the oven at 425°F.

Hardcook six of the eggs. Separate the seventh, lightly beat the yolk and add it to the cream or milk.

Roll out pastry thinly and cut out circles measuring 6 inches in diameter, using a saucer or small plate as a guide. Roll out pork on a floured board and cut into six equal pieces. Place a hardcooked egg on each piece of pork and, with the tips of your fingers dipped into the unbeaten egg white, work the pork around the egg until the egg is completely enclosed.

Dip each egg shape into egg white, then roll up in pastry until completely enclosed. Place on a floured cookie sheet. Brush with egg yolk and milk glaze and bake in the preset oven until golden brown — about 15–20 minutes. Serve when cooled, cut into portions.

Tartlets Niçoise

basic shortcrust pastry made
from 2 cups flour
8–10 button mushrooms
1 medium onion
½ clove of garlic
1 large red pepper
2 tomatoes
2 zucchini
1 small eggplant
2–3 tbsp oil and a little extra oil
Parmesan cheese (optional)
salt and pepper

Set the oven at 350°F.

Wash mushrooms, but keep whole. Peel and chop onion; core and deseed pepper and cut into small dice. Crush garlic with a little salt. Deseed tomatoes and roughly chop; slice zucchini; cut eggplant into dice. Line chosen tartlet molds with pastry. Bake tartlet molds blind in preset oven for 15 to 20 minutes, until browned and cooked. Meanwhile, heat oil in pan, add onion, garlic, pepper, zucchini and eggplant. Season and simmer gently until well cooked and very soft. Sauté the mushrooms separately.

Fill the cases, place a mushroom on top and sprinkle with Parmesan cheese.

Canapés and hors d'oeuvres

Salmon Asparagus Rolls are delightful for more sophisticated occasions.

Salmon Asparagus Rolls

¼ lb smoked salmon cut into slices
1 small can asparagus tips, or fresh
    asparagus if available

For garnish
thick basic mayonnaise
lemon wedges
parsley sprigs

Drain asparagus tips and pat dry on absorbent paper, or cook and drain if fresh. Roll each tip in a slice of smoked salmon and place the rolls on a serving dish. With a pastry bag and star pipe, pipe rosettes of mayonnaise on each roll to garnish. Surround with lemon wedges and sprigs of parsley.

As a variation, serve the salmon asparagus rolls with the mayonnaise in a bowl, so that guests may dip their rolls.

It is often possible to buy cheaper scraps of smoked salmon from the ends of a piece. Use the larger pieces for this recipe and the remains to make a mousse or a smoked salmon pâté.

Caviare Stuffed Tomatoes and Shrimp Boats.

Caviare Stuffed Tomatoes

12 small tomatoes
1¼ cups heavy cream
1 small jar or can caviare or lumpfish roe
2 tsp lemon juice
browned almonds to garnish (optional)
salt
freshly ground black pepper

Place tomatoes in very hot water for a few moments to split the skin and make it easy to remove. Peel tomatoes. Whip cream.

Slice the tops off the tomatoes from the flower end. Remove and discard seeds, and turn each tomato upside down to drain. Drain and stir the caviare or lumpfish roe into the whipped cream and then, very carefully, add the lemon juice to flavor the cream. Season to taste with salt and black pepper.

Place tomatoes upright on a serving dish and, with a pastry bag and plain pipe – or use a small teaspoon – fill each tomato case. Replace tops and garnish with flaked browned almonds, if liked.

Lumpfish roe is often known as poor man's caviare. It is delicious, and much cheaper than caviare itself!

Shrimp Boats

basic savory shortcrust pastry
    made from 1 cup flour
¼ pt peeled and veined shrimps
¼–⅜ cup heavy cream
¼ cup basic mayonnaise
pinch of cayenne pepper
1 tsp lemon juice
1 egg
1 or 2 drops anchovy flavoring
black pepper
chopped parsley

Roll out pastry and line into the smallest boat molds. (The exact number made depends on the size of your molds.) Bake blind for a few minutes at 375°F. Allow to cool. Whip heavy cream. Hardcook egg and, when cool, sieve white and yolk together.

Fold heavy cream into mayonnaise, add the sieved egg and then the shrimps. Season to taste with cayenne, lemon juice, anchovy flavoring and black pepper. Pile mixture into boatshaped pastry cases. Garnish with a little parsley.

Roquefort Puffs are ideal bites to serve with drinks.

Roquefort Puffs

For cheese choux pastry
6 tbsp butter or margarine
⅓ cup milk
1 cup flour
a little ground nutmeg
¼ cup grated Parmesan cheese
3 eggs
black pepper

For filling
¼ lb Roquefort cheese
¼ cup sweet butter
2 tbsp port
freshly ground black pepper

For garnish
flaked almonds
watercress

Make up the pastry, by putting butter and milk together in a thick based pan over low heat, and stir until the milk boils. Add flour all at once, and remove pan from heat. Add nutmeg, and cheese and season with black pepper. Beat vigorously with a wooden spoon until smooth, and the mixture leaves the side of the pan and looks more like dough. Add an egg and continue beating until smooth again. Add the second egg and continue beating until mixture is smooth. Add the third egg and beat again. Leave until cold before filling mixture into a pastry bag with a plain round pipe – approximately ½ inch in diameter, and pipe small buns onto an oiled cookie sheet.

Bake in the oven at 425°F for 25–30 minutes, then prick with a skewer to release any steam and keep the pastry crisp. Fill when cool.

To make the filling, beat the cheese with the butter until smooth. Add port and beat again until thoroughly blended in. Season with black pepper to taste and spoon mixture into a pastry bag with a star pipe attached. Cut lids from the cooled choux pastry buns and, if necessary, cut out any soggy pastry in the center. Fill each bun with Roquefort mixture and sprinkle with the flaked almonds. Garnish with the watercress and chill slightly before serving.

Canapés and hors d'oeuvres

Russian Salad Butterflies

scraps or small amount basic savory shortcrust pastry

For filling
diced, cooked mixed vegetables – carrots, peas, green beans, potatoes
basic mayonnaise

For garnish
paprika
cucumber strips (optional)

Set the oven at 375°F.

Roll out pastry scraps and cut into rounds, each measuring 2½ inches in diameter. Allow two rounds per butterfly and cut one of these in half. Bake in the preset oven until golden brown and cooked.

Add sufficient mayonnaise to the cooked vegetables to form a firm mixture and spoon about 1 tbsp onto each round. Place the two pastry halves on the mixture to form wings, and sprinkle a little paprika across the join.

As a variation, cut the pastry with an oval cookie cutter, and when adding the wings, disguise the join with a strip of cucumber.

This is a perfect recipe for using up leftover vegetables, but if you have none available, substitute canned or ready-made vegetable salad.

Egg Cocotte Tartlets

For each tartlet
scraps of basic savory shortcrust pastry
1 tbsp cooked spinach (optional)
small slice cooked ham
1 egg
butter or margarine
1 tbsp light cream
2 tbsp grated Cheddar cheese
grated nutmeg (optional)
salt and pepper

Set the oven at 375°F.

Roll out the scraps of pastry and cut out each tartlet 3 inches in diameter. Line into molds and bake blind in the preset oven until golden brown and cooked.

When tartlet case is cooked, place the spinach at the base of the case. Add the slice of cooked ham, trimming off the sides a little if necessary. Poach the egg in a little butter or margarine, using an egg poacher or a 2 inch diameter cookie cutter as a mold inside the pan of simmering water to keep it in shape. (In this case do not let the water come up over the sides of the cutter, and dot the top of the egg with a little butter).

When cooked, slide the egg onto the tartlet, pour over cream, sprinkle with cheese, season to taste, adding nutmeg if liked, and slide under a hot broiler to melt the cheese and brown it a little. Serve hot.

Egg Cocotte Tartlets make a good savory supper snack for smaller gatherings. Have everything prepared so that you only need to poach the eggs.

Latticed Shrimp Tartlets

For each tartlet
scraps of basic savory shortcrust pastry
1 tbsp basic thick white sauce
1 tbsp chopped, peeled and veined shrimps
½–1 cap of canned pimiento
salt and pepper

Set the oven at 375°F.

Roll out the scraps of pastry and cut with a 3 inch diameter cutter. Line into mold and bake blind in the preset oven until golden brown and cooked. Allow to cool. Make up basic white sauce, if not using leftover sauce.

Stir chopped shrimps into basic white sauce. Season to taste and pile into baked pastry case. Cut pimiento cap into very fine strips and lay across surface of tartlet to make a lattice pattern. Serve cold.

Cheese Boats

basic savory shortcrust pastry made from 1 cup flour
3 slices processed cheese
half an 8 oz package cream cheese
2 tbsp chopped celery
paprika
¼ cup milk or light cream

Set the oven at 375°F.

Make up shortcrust pastry, if not already in freezer. Roll out and line into small boat shaped molds. Cut processed cheese slices into triangles.

Beat the chopped celery into the cream cheese and flavor with a little cayenne pepper, if liked. Fill into boat molds and add a few drops of milk or cream to each. Bake in the preset oven for 7–10 minutes or until pastry is golden brown and cooked. When cooled, add a triangular sail of processed cheese, secured with a small cocktail pick or toothpick, if necessary. Serve warm.

As a finishing touch, if desired, dip the sails in paprika.

White Sauce

Basic Recipe

¼ cup butter or margarine
¾ cup flour
2½ cups hot milk
salt and pepper

Melt the butter or margarine in a pan. Stir in the flour with a wooden spoon and cook gently for 1–2 minutes until the mixture forms a soft ball, stirring constantly.

Remove pan from heat and gradually stir in the hot milk, beating vigorously all the time to obtain a smooth sauce. When all the milk is incorporated, return pan to heat and gently bring to the boil. Stir for 3–4 minutes.

Remove from heat and use immediately, or cover sauce with a piece of dampened waxed paper and leave until required. Reheat gently before serving.

This quantity makes 2½ cups of thick coating sauce. For a thinner pouring sauce, use 3 tbsp butter or margarine and ¼ cup + 1 tbsp flour to 2½ cups milk.

Mornay (Cheese) Sauce

Basic Recipe

1 cup butter or margarine
½ cup flour
2½ cups hot milk
½–¾ cup grated cheese
¼ tsp ground mace or nutmeg
salt and pepper

Melt the butter or margarine in a pan. Stir in the flour with a wooden spoon and cook gently for 1–2 minutes until the mixture forms a soft ball, stirring constantly.

Remove pan from heat and gradually stir in the hot milk, beating vigorously all the time to obtain a smooth sauce. When all the milk is incorporated, return pan to heat and bring to the boil, stirring all

Potato Nests, garnished with chopped chives.

the time to keep the sauce smooth.

Lower the heat and add the cheese and seasonings. Simmer gently until the sauce thickens, stirring constantly. Remove from heat and use immediately, or cover sauce with a piece of dampened waxed paper and leave until required. Reheat gently before serving.

Use Cheddar cheese if a mild flavor is liked, Parmesan or Gruyère for a stronger flavor.

Potato Nests

2 large or 4 medium potatoes
6 tbsp butter or margarine
¼ cup cooking oil
lemon juice
chopped chives or parsley to garnish
salt and pepper

Peel potatoes, pat dry and cut into matchstick slices, or use a mandoline grater.

Heat oil and butter, or margarine, in a heavy frypan over low heat. Take a handful of the grated potato and shape into a flat nest. Sprinkle over a few drops of lemon juice and sauté the potato nests on both sides until cooked, crisp and browned. Lift from pan with a slotted spoon and drain on absorbent paper, then season with salt and pepper and sprinkle with chopped chives or parsley to garnish. Make other nests in the same way until potato is used up. Serve hot.

To make the potato nests really brown and crisp, drain off most of the cooking fat or oil and finish off sautéing in just a little fat.

This is an economical way of serving potatoes. The only problem is that this recipe is so delicious that your guests will eat double quantity at least!

Low-cholesterol or slimmers margarines are not recommended for frying, as their water content is high. It is better to stick to butter and oil mixed, or ordinary margarine for the best effect.

Canapés and hors d'oeuvres

Mushroom Savories (Mock Snails)

1 cup mushrooms
basic garlic butter
2 1-inch thick slices of white bread
1⅓ cups fresh white breadcrumbs
½ cup finely ground almonds
salt and pepper

Set the oven at 350°F.

Wash and chop the mushrooms very finely. Make garlic butter, if none in stock. Cut bread cubes by trimming off crusts from bread slices and cutting neat 1 inch cubes. You will need about 16 cubes.

In a bowl, mix together the chopped mushrooms, breadcrumbs and almonds.

Season with salt and pepper. Using either tiny individual ovenproof pots – allow four per person – or individual ovenproof ramekin dishes – allow one per person – spoon the mixture into the pots.

Melt the garlic butter over low heat and pour enough over each pot or ramekin to thoroughly moisten the mushroom mixture. Balance a cube of bread on each tiny pot, or allow 3–4 cubes for each ramekin.

Place pots on a cookie sheet and bake in the preset oven for about 10–15 minutes for the tiny pots and 15 minutes for the ramekins.

Garlic Butter

2–3 cloves of garlic
¼ cup butter
2 tbsp chopped parsley
1 level tsp salt

Peel and finely chop the garlic. Crush with the salt in a mortar with a pestle. Cream the butter in a separate bowl, then add the garlic and the chopped parsley. Beat together until thoroughly mixed. Chill before using.

Eggs à la Russe

10 eggs
3 inch length of cucumber
1 small jar or can lumpfish roe
2 tbsp heavy cream

To garnish
strips of pimiento or tomato

Hardcook eggs. Cut cucumber into slices each ½ inch thick. Canelle the edges first, if liked, to decorate. Whip cream stiffly.

Peel the eggs and halve lengthwise. Mash yolks with drained lumpfish roe and bind with whipped cream. Refill eggs, sandwich together in pairs and place each upright on a cucumber base. Decorate with tiny strips of pimiento or tomato to disguise the join.

Cheese Straws

basic puff pastry made from 1 cup flour
scant ½ cup strong flavored cheese (or ¼ cup
    Parmesan, if possible)
2 tbsp butter or margarine
cayenne pepper
poppy seeds to garnish (optional)
salt and pepper

Set the oven at 425°F.

Make up the pastry, if none is in the freezer. Grate the cheese. Melt the butter or margarine.

Roll out the puff pastry very thinly into a rectangle. Brush lightly with melted butter or margarine and sprinkle over most of the grated cheese. Season with just a pinch of cayenne pepper, and salt and pepper, then fold the pastry over and roll it out again thickly. Slice pastry into strips, each

Mushroom Savories or Mock Snails with Garlic Butter.

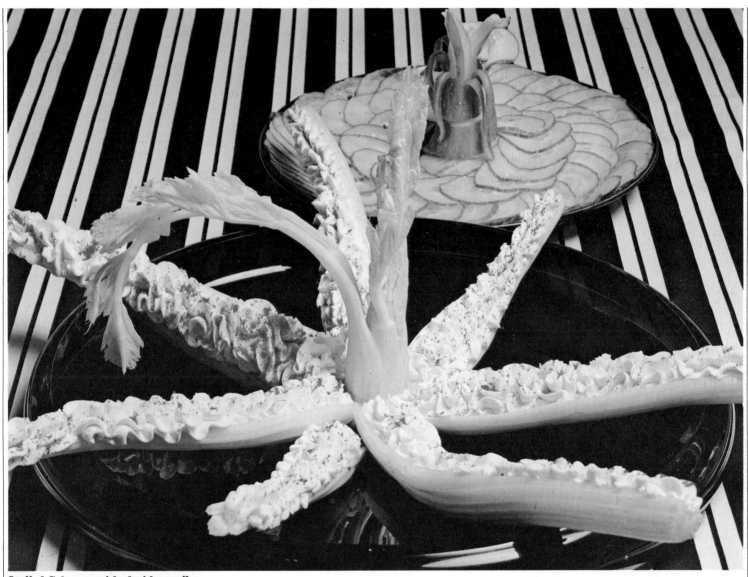

Stuffed Celery garnished with paprika.

about 6 inches long, and ¾ inch wide. Twist each strip and place on a floured cookie sheet, brushing each one with a little more melted butter or margarine and sprinkling over the remaining grated cheese.

Bake in the preset oven for 10–12 minutes until golden brown and crisp. Serve immediately, sprinkled with poppy seeds, if liked.

Stuffed Celery

celery stalks
paprika

For filling
¼ cup heavy cream
3 oz package cream cheese
dry sherry to taste
pinch of celery salt
pinch of cayenne pepper
salt and pepper

Wash and dry the celery stalks. Lightly whip the cream and beat it into the cheese.

Add sherry to taste and season with salt, pepper and celery salt.

Spoon the mixture into a pastry bag, and using a large star nozzle, pipe the cream cheese filling into the celery stalks. Sprinkle with paprika before serving.

For more individual servings, cut the stuffed celery into 2 inch long pieces and arrange on a dish.

This is a delightful canapé to serve at summer buffet parties.

Canapés and hors d'oeuvres

Buffet Table Eggs

Eggs make very satisfying hors d'oeuvres and appetizers, especially when served cold for summer buffets. Try some of the following variations.

Variation 1

scraps of basic puff pastry
6 eggs
4–5 tbsp basic mayonnaise
juice of ½ lemon
Tabasco sauce (optional)

For garnish
sprigs of parsley
grated rind of ½ orange (optional)

Set the oven at 425°F.

Roll out the pastry and cut into six rounds about 2 inches in diameter with a cookie cutter. Bake in the preset oven until golden brown and cooked.

Hardcook the eggs. Flavor three-quarters of the mayonnaise with lemon juice to taste. Peel the eggs, slice off enough of the base so that the yolk of each can be spooned out. Mash the yolk with the lemon flavored mayonnaise and add a few drops of Tabasco, if liked. Take care not to make the mayonnaise too thin as it will seep out from the base of the stuffed egg. Place spoonfulls of the mixture into the eggs and place each on a puff pastry base.

Flavor the rest of the basic mayonnaise with a little grated orange rind, if desired, or leave plain. Pipe small rosettes of mayonnaise around the base of each egg to decorate. Top each egg with a sprig of parsley.

Variation 2

3 small oranges
6 eggs
3 tbsp basic mayonnaise
strips of orange rind

For filling
2–3 oz pâté
1–2 tbsp light cream
dry sherry or brandy, to taste
salt and pepper

Cut oranges around with deep v-shaped cuts, then hollow out by removing the orange flesh. Add a few strips of orange rind to flavor the mayonnaise. Hardcook the eggs. Cream the pâté by adding cream and brandy or sherry and mixing thoroughly. Season.

Peel the eggs, slice off a little from the base of each egg. Scoop out the yolk and mash with creamed pâté. Fill the eggs with the mixture and place each egg inside an orange cup. Pipe small rosettes of orange flavored mayonnaise between the spikes of the oranges to decorate. Cut the slice of egg into a fancy shape and top the egg with this.

Variation 3

6 eggs
6 vol-au-vent cases
2 tbsp basic cheese sauce
3 tbsp of cooked peas
a little basic aspic

Softcook the eggs by gently lowering into a pan of boiling water. Leave to cook for 4 minutes, then pour off water and replace with cold. Peel carefully by first of all tapping the shell of the egg all over with a teaspoon. Then peel off a band of shell round the middle. The two ends should then come away with the gentlest of twists. Make up the cheese sauce, if necessary.

Into each vol-au-vent case, first place a tsp basic cheese sauce, then a softcooked egg. Pour a tablespoon or two of aspic on the point of setting over each egg. Surround each one with a ring of cooked peas and coat with a little more aspic. Leave to set.

Variation 4

3 eggs
1 loaf white bread
anchovy paste
2 tbsp sweet butter
1–2 tbsp grated Parmesan cheese
English mustard powder
1 tbsp heavy cream
gherkins to garnish

Cut slices of bread ¼ inch thick from the loaf, stamp out 2 inch circles (about 6) with a cookie cutter and fry in a little butter or oil until golden brown. Drain on absorbent paper. Hardcook eggs. Whip cream.

Spread each fried bread croûte with a little anchovy paste mixed up with 2 tbsp of sweet butter. Peel and halve eggs lengthwise, scoop out yolks. Mix the yolks with the grated Parmesan, a pinch of mustard powder and bind with the heavy cream.

Place a tsp of the mixture inside each halved egg and put the halves, cut side downward, on the prepared bread croûte. Garnish with gherkins, if liked.

Variation 5

6 bread croûtes (see Variation 4)
6 eggs
¾ cup peeled and veined shrimps
¾ cup basic mayonnaise
a few drops of lemon juice

Fry bread croûtes; hardcook eggs. Flavor basic mayonnaise with lemon juice to taste. Pound shrimps to a purée.

Peel and halve eggs lengthwise. Scoop out yolks, sieve them and add to mayonnaise. Add pounded shrimps and mix well. Carefully spoon or pipe the mixture into the halved eggs, and place the halves in upright pairs on a bread croûte. Pipe or spoon a little extra mixture between stuffed egg halves to hold them together.

Variation 6

4 eggs
6 medium tomatoes
1 tsp onion juice
3–4 tbsp cream cheese
¼ tsp celery salt
2 tbsp heavy cream
a few stuffed green olives

Hardcook eggs. Scald and skin tomatoes, cut off the tops at the flower end and scoop out the seeds. Turn upside down to drain.

Peel eggs, remove yolks and mash together with the onion juice, cream cheese, celery salt and bind with cream to make a firm consistency. Chop up most of the egg white finely and add this.

Fill each tomato with the mixture, forming the top into a mound. Garnish, if liked, with a little reserved egg white, cut into a fancy shape. Top each with a slice of stuffed green olive. Otherwise, replace tomato lids.

It is difficult to give precise quantities for these egg fillings. Much depends on the size of the eggs, and the size of the tomatoes. Adjust quantities to suit.

Some of the many ways of serving Buffet Eggs.

Canapés and hors d'oeuvres

Austrian Liptauer Cheese

½ an 8 oz package cream cheese
½ cup sweet butter
1 generous tsp paprika
caraway seeds
5 capers
1 anchovy fillet
1 tsp prepared French mustard
salt and pepper

Put butter in a warm place to soften; chop caraway seeds; drain and chop capers finely; soak anchovy fillet in a little milk to remove excess saltiness, then chop.

Beat warmed butter until light and fluffy, then beat in the cream cheese slowly. When mixture is smooth, add paprika, caraway seeds, capers, chopped anchovy fillet and mustard. Continue beating. Taste for seasoning and adjust, if necessary.

Shape into a rectangle or square and chill before serving on triangles of brown toast, dark rye bread, pumpernickel or pretzel biscuits.

This is an Austrian version of the classic Hungarian recipe. Chopped chives, or garlic or finely chopped onion are alternatives to add as variations.

Liptauer cheese is good spread quickly over warmed crackers, if rye bread etc. is not available.

Carrot Boats

basic shortcrust pastry made from 1 cup
  flour
¼ lb new carrots
⅛–¼ cup heavy cream
1 tbsp butter or margarine
nutmeg
a few black olives for garnish
salt and black pepper

Set the oven at 375°F.

Peel carrots and boil in salted water until thoroughly cooked. Make up pastry, line into boat molds and bake blind in the preset oven for a few minutes, until pastry is golden brown and cooked. Whip up cream.

Drain cooked carrots and mash well with a fork, or pass through a blender or Mouli-sieve. Beat in the butter, or margarine, season with nutmeg, salt and pepper and fold in the whipped cream.

Pile carrot mixture into pastry cases, decorate each with a slice or two of black olive and serve, preferably hot.

Stuffed Artichoke Hearts

1 small can artichoke hearts
4–5 tbsp basic thick cheese sauce
1 tbsp butter or margarine
1 tomato
a little hardcooked egg white (optional)

Make up cheese sauce and keep hot. Peel tomato, cut flesh into strips, using pinking shears to trim, if liked. Discard seeds. Chop up egg white.

Heat artichoke hearts gently in a little of the juice from the can. Then drain hearts, place on a heatproof serving dish and fill each with a tbsp of thick cheese sauce. Dot each with butter and slide under the broiler so the surface bubbles and slightly browns. Garnish each with a strip of tomato and a little hardcooked egg white. Serve hot.

An additional garnish of fried onion rings can be added for those not dieting.

Use fresh artichokes if they are available and fill the scooped-out center with the filling.

Austrian Liptauer Cheese garnished with pretzel biscuits.

Carrot Boats, Stuffed Mushrooms and Stuffed Artichoke Hearts.

Stuffed Mushrooms

1 lb fresh medium mushrooms
½ cup Madeira, port or cream sherry
½ cup concentrated chicken stock or
 consommé
fried or toasted croûtons

For filling
⅔ cup heavy cream
1 × 1½ oz jar lumpfish roe
2 tsp lemon juice
freshly ground black pepper

Wipe the mushrooms clean with a damp cloth, but do not peel. Discard stalks. Put mushroom caps in a large skillet, dome side uppermost. Pour in the Madeira, port or sherry and the stock or consommé and simmer over low heat for about 4 minutes.

Turn the mushrooms over carefully with cooking tongs and simmer for another 2–3 minutes. Transfer to a serving platter with a slotted spoon, arranging them dome side down.

Continue to simmer the liquid in the pan until reduced to a syrupy consistency, then pour over the mushrooms. Set aside.

Whip the cream until thick. Fold in the lumpfish roe until evenly blended, then gently blend in the lemon juice with black pepper to taste.

Spoon or pipe the prepared filling into the mushroom caps and chill in the refrigerator until serving time. Garnish the platter with croûtons just before serving.

Serve Savory Pimiento croûtes hot or chilled.

Savory Pimiento Croûtes

generous 1 lb red and green peppers
½ lb onions
scant ¼ cup cooking oil
1 level tsp ginger
1 lb tomatoes
¾ cup light brown sugar
⅔ cup raisins or seedless raisins
1 generous tsp mixed spice
1 clove garlic, crushed with a little salt
1¼ cups wine vinegar
1 tsp dried tarragon

To serve
bread croûtes

Set the oven at 300°F.

Peel and finely chop the onions. Remove core and seeds from peppers and chop into dice.

Heat oil in a pan and add the peppers and onions. Fry gently over a low heat until onions are transparent. Cover and simmer for about 8 minutes.

Add the remaining ingredients, stir gently until mixed, then cover and simmer until thoroughly cooked and mushy. Cook for a further 10 minutes without the lid to evaporate the excess juices.

To prepare the croûtes, cut rounds from 3 or 4 slices of white bread with a 3 inch cutter. Fry rounds in a little oil or butter until golden brown and crisp, drain on absorbent paper before serving.

Strain off any excess juices from the mixture and pile on top of prepared bread croûtes. Serve hot or chilled.

French Dressing

¼ tsp salt
¼ tsp finely ground
   black pepper
¼ tsp prepared
   French mustard
⅔ cup olive or corn oil
4 tbsp wine vinegar

Put the salt, pepper and mustard in a salad bowl with a little oil. Beat with a wooden spoon or fork until thick. Add the remaining oil gradually, beating it in alternately with the wine vinegar. Taste for seasoning and add more salt if too oily. Beat again to combine before tossing salad vegetables.

The dressing can be made quickly by putting all ingredients in a screw topped jar and shaking vigorously. Store in the refrigerator and use as required.

This is a classic recipe for French dressing; for a classic vinaigrette mix in 2 tsp finely chopped herbs, shallot or onion before serving.

Mayonnaise

1 egg yolk
¼ tsp dry mustard
salt and pepper
⅔ cup olive
   or corn oil
1 tbsp lemon juice
   or wine vinegar

It is essential to keep mixing bowl and utensils cool and all ingredients should be at room temperature. Add the oil very slowly at first, or the mayonnaise will curdle.

Put the egg yolk, mustard and salt and pepper to taste in a bowl. Beat with a wooden spoon, electric or rotary beater until well mixed. Add the oil a drop at a time, beating well all the time. Beat in the oil faster when the mayonnaise thickens, then add the lemon juice or wine vinegar. Beat until well mixed and taste for seasoning. Cover and store in a cool place until required.

If mayonnaise curdles, start again with a fresh egg yolk. Beat the curdled mayonnaise into the egg yolk a drop at a time until the mixture becomes thick, then add remaining oil.

Bouchées à la Grecque

1 cup large dry Lima beans
1 medium onion
2 cloves garlic
dash powdered coriander
8 slices white bread from
   a sandwich loaf
1 tsp baking soda
salt and pepper
chopped parsley to garnish

Soak the Lima beans overnight. Remove crusts from slices of bread and soak bread for a few minutes. Peel onion and garlic.

Pass soaked beans through a grinder or Mouli-sieve, with the onion and garlic. Pound with a pestle in a mortar with the soaked bread, or use a blender, to achieve a smooth "dough". Pound in, or add, coriander and baking soda, season and chill mixture for 2 hours. Roll into small balls and deep fry until golden and crisp. Drain on absorbent paper and serve on cocktail picks. Sprinkle with chopped parsley, if wished.

Bouchées à la Grecque can be served with a variety of dips.

29

Canapés and hors d'oeuvres

Canapé Suggestions

Fish
Anchovy Matchsticks: Roll out basic puff pastry made from 1 cup flour thinly, cut into rectangles, and lay an anchovy fillet (previously soaked in milk to remove excess saltiness) along each. Brush edges with beaten egg, fold over and press all around to seal. Brush tops with egg and milk glaze and bake in the oven at 425°F for 10–12 minutes.

Anchovy Canapés: Spread fried croûtes of bread with sweet butter flavored with anchovy flavoring or paste to taste, then garnish with a slice of skinned tomato and a black pitted olive.

Shrimp Croûtes: In a mortar with a pestle, pound fresh or frozen shelled shrimps with an equal quantity of sweet butter. Spread the paste on fried croûtes of bread, sprinkle each with a little sieved hard-cooked egg yolk. Top with a tiny pat of butter and garnish with whole shrimps.

Angels on Horseback: For each, wrap an oyster in a small rasher of bacon and broil. Place on a small rectangle of fresh buttered toast and season very lightly with a tiny pinch of cayenne pepper.

Salmon Tartlets: Fill baked savory shortcrust pastry cases with a little basic thick cheese sauce, into which cooked, flaked salmon has been mixed. Sprinkle each with grated Parmesan and broil to brown the tops before serving.

'Caviare' Canapés: Spread croûtes or slices of bread with butter, then add a generous tsp of Danish 'lumpfish' roe to each. Serve with a sprinkling of lemon juice from wedges garnishing the serving dish.

'Caviare' Choux: Bake tiny puffs of basic choux pastry and when cool, split each and fill with a little black caviare or lumpfish roe, folded into a little whipped cream to bind. Add a generous squeeze of lemon juice to flavor, and a little freshly ground black pepper.

Meat
Rissoles (Pomponettes): Grind cold cooked poultry or game and bind with a little basic thick cheese sauce. Shape into small sausages and chill. When firm, roll first in beaten egg, then breadcrumbs, and deep fry until golden brown and cooked.

'Pâté' Choux: Bake tiny puffs of basic choux pastry and, when cool, split each and fill with chicken liver pâté, folded into

Some suggestions for serving and garnishing canapés.

whipped cream, flavored with a little sherry.

Tartelettes Agnès Sorel: Fill tartlet cases with ground cooked chicken, or chicken and ground tongue, bound with basic cheese or basic white sauce and a little whipped cream. Season with salt and pepper.

Sausage Savories: Broil cocktail-size sausages and serve each on a croûte of fried bread, garnished with fried onion rings.

Bouchées à la Reine: Fill small vol-au-vent cases with finely diced or ground cooked meat or poultry and cooked mushrooms, bound together with enough basic thick white sauce.

Cheese
Cheese Canapés: Spread finger-size croûtes of fried bread with thick basic cheese sauce. Sprinkle tops with a little melted butter and brown under the broiler.

Cheese Matchsticks: Roll out basic puff pastry made from 1 cup of flour thinly, cut into small rectangles, brush with beaten egg and sprinkle half of each generously with Parmesan cheese, finishing with a pinch of cayenne pepper. Fold over halves, press edges to seal and brush tops with egg and milk glaze. Bake at 400°F for about 10 minutes.

Cheese Boats: Make small boat shaped cases of basic savory shortcrust pastry and bake the pastry before adding the filling. When cool, fill with basic thick cheese sauce flavored with grated Parmesan cheese and with a little stiffly whipped cream folded in when the sauce is cool. Sprinkle with extra Parmesan.

Cheese Choux: Make tiny puffs of basic choux pastry, bake and when cool, split and fill with the basic thick cheese sauce as described for Cheese Boats.

Egg
Egg Canapés: Spread circles of brown bread with butter, a little basic thick mayonnaise and add a sprinkling of chopped hardcooked egg. Garnish with chopped cress or parsley.

Sandwich Suggestions

Fish

Thinly sliced pickled sea herring with equally thinly sliced onion rings and a little horseradish sauce.

Smoked sea herring with hardcooked egg slices and a little mayonnaise or horseradish sauce.

Smoked haddock, flaked and mixed with a little basic thick cheese sauce. Add a little whipped cream to the sauce for better flavor and consistency.

Poached salmon, flaked and mixed into a little basic orange mayonnaise.

Cods' roe pâté, well-seasoned with pepper and a little extra lemon juice.

Lumpfish roe or Danish caviare on open sandwiches, with a little basic mayonnaise or herb butter and a squeeze of lemon juice.

Shrimps or prawns, shelled and veined and chopped and mixed with basic mayonnaise, sharpened with a drop or two of Tabasco sauce.

Anchovy flavoring, beaten into sweet butter to taste, with shelled, veined and chopped shrimps or prawns.

Meat

Potted or pressed beef, mixed with chopped cucumber, tomatoes and a chopped cap of canned pimiento, bound with basic thick mayonnaise, flavored with a pinch or two of curry powder.

Cold roast pork, chopped and folded into whipped cream, into which a little jelly from the joint has been mixed.

Slices of crisp cooked bacon, derinded and spread with pork dripping and topped with lettuce and tomatoes to garnish.

Cooked ham, diced and mixed with a spinach purée; a spreading consistency – and extra flavor – is achieved by beating in a little cream cheese and salt and pepper.

Skinned and chopped fresh, country-style pork sausages, mixed with chopped hardcooked egg and mixed thoroughly with basic mayonnaise to bind. Add a little basic French dressing, if liked, as an extra.

Cooked chicken, shredded or diced, bound with tomato-flavored mayonnaise and sprinkled with chopped watercress.

Cheese

Cream cheese, beaten smooth and flavored with a little sherry, crushed walnuts and diced celery.

Stuffed Olive Croûtes

3–4½ inch thick slices of white bread
1 egg
scant ½ cup milk
15 pitted black olives
15 pitted green olives
oil or fat for frying
half an 8 oz package cream cheese
celery salt
chopped parsley to garnish
black pepper

Cut 24 small rounds of bread about 1½ inches diameter from the bread slices with a fluted cutter. Beat the egg well and add to the milk. Make sure the olives really are pitted.

Dip the bread rounds in the egg and milk mixture and fry quickly in a small amount of heated oil or fat until golden brown and crisp. Drain well on absorbent paper.

In a bowl, beat the cream cheese until soft, season with a pinch of celery salt and freshly ground black pepper. Fill into a pastry bag fitted with a small star pipe, and pipe a rosette of cream cheese in and on top of each of 12 black and 12 green olives, reserving 3 of each for garnish.

Arrange fried bread croûtes on a plate, place a generous spot of cream cheese on each. Surround with chopped parsley and stand a stuffed olive on each. Cut each reserved olive into four, and place a slice of olive on each cream cheese rosette. Serve chilled.

A little heavy cream beaten into the cream cheese before piping will help if the cheese remains too thick to pipe. Be careful not to add too much, or the mixture will be too thin to pipe.

Savory Pinwheels

These are always popular party canapés, and are easy to make. Trim all crusts off a standard, unsliced brown or white loaf and butter the top of the long side. Cut loaf into slices lengthwise, buttering each first. It is easier to do this if the loaf is fresh by dipping a straight-edged knife into boiling water, wiping it quickly and then using. Warm the knife blade in this way before each slice is cut.

Spread each slice with any of the fillings in Sandwich Suggestions and roll up. Now wrap each one tightly in a layer of foil or waxed paper and chill in the refrigerator. Just before serving, cut in thin slices.

Stuffed Olive Croûtes.

HOW TO CANELLE AND GARNISH

1. To cut gherkin tassels: Simply make a lengthwise cut down the center almost to the opposite tip of the gherkin, but be careful not to cut completely through. Then cut as many lengthwise slices as possible from sides to the middle. Fan out into a tassel.

2. To cut tomato roses: Peel a tomato just as you would an apple, in one long strip. With skin side inwards, roll round into a 'flower' shape. Pinch the base to keep it firm. Use another length of peel to make further layers of 'petals' if necessary.

Clever Garnishing Tricks for Savories

Garnishes aim to stimulate the appetite and enhance the color and appearance of the dish. Simple garnishes are often the most effective – a crisp bunch of watercress, a slice of lemon or a sprinkling of parsley, but with a sharp vegetable knife or a special canelle knife, you can create some more professional and attractive garnishes.

The sharp vegetable knife can be used to make very thin slices of any vegetables and fruit. Try cutting thin slices of cucumber and then cutting each slice from the edge to the center. Twist one cut edge away from the center and make the slices stand up. Try notching oranges or lemons, by cutting a band of 'V's around the middle. Another idea is to make brushes with celery or scallions. With celery, cut stalks into 2 inch lengths. Cut thin slices down each end and place in ice water to curl. For scallions, cut off the root and trim the stalk to make 2 inch lengths. Cut thin slivers through both ends and place in iced water to curl.

The canelle knife has a notch in one side which is used to shape fruit and vegetables. Many of the examples show the shapes that can be made with the canelle knife. Add extra touches with olives and parsley. Orange and lemon twists are most effective to decorate the edges of a serving dish.

3. To make carrot shapes: Peel and cut carrots into neat slices. If you do not have a set of tiny cutters in different shapes (e.g. hearts, petals, etc), try using as cutters the tiny French 'petit four' molds available at most specialist shops.

Some examples given:
top: two types of carrot flower; (left) with saw-tooth edge, a black olive center and scallion or chive 'stalks', (right) petals cut with a round cutter, with a slice of stuffed green olive in the center.
center: two more types of carrot flowers; (left) petals are scalloped with a sharp vegetable knife and the center is, again, a slice of stuffed green olive; (right) a vegetable flower made from a scalloped round with a carrot that has had the spaces between the petal pieces shaved out of it.
3rd row: tiny hearts cut with a special cutter.
4th row: cut each little heart in half; reverse one half and this 'wings' shape is the result.

4. Take a small orange and using the canelle knife cut around the fruit. Start at the stem end and cut in a continuous strip to the base, giving the orange a striped effect. Use the canelled orange as a decoration and the strips of orange peel to garnish the dish.

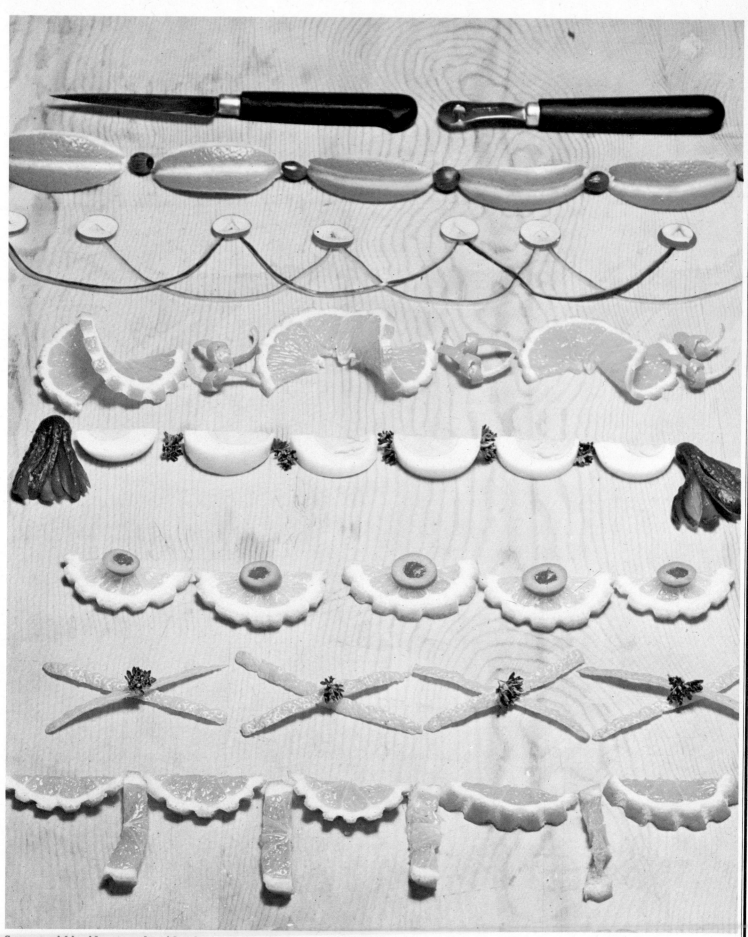

Some garnishing ideas to make with a sharp vegetable knife and a canelle knife.
From the top, orange segments with pickled onions, strip of cucumber peel, canelled twists of orange,
slices of hardcooked egg with gherkin tassells, and some lemon and orange ideas.

Cold appetizers

The most successful dinner parties and buffets are often those where the hostess has prepared many of the dishes in advance and can concentrate her attention on her guests. Cold appetizers or starters are therefore often the salvation of the busy hostess, as many of them can be prepared early and chilled until required. A final touch of dressing or some garnishing is all that is required before serving.

The starter should tempt the palate for things to come, so don't fall into the trap of serving large helpings with too rich dressings or sauces. The emphasis should be on natural flavors. Choose one main ingredient, such as lobster, salmon, avocado pears, mushrooms, or grapefruit for the best effect. There is no need to be nervous about using expensive ingredients with which you are unfamiliar, as there are step-by-step instructions for preparing shellfish such as lobster and crab and vegetables such as globe artichokes.

The following dishes give a wide choice of appetizers, for both the formal and the informal gathering. Some can be prepared in a few minutes, while the more elaborate require a little advance planning. And many of the dishes may give you ideas for main courses.

A wealth of seafood.

34

Preparing a Live Lobster

1 carrot
1 onion
5 cups water
¼ cup wine vinegar
1 small sprig of thyme
1 small bay leaf
2 black peppercorns
live lobster

Make a court bouillon as follows. Peel and grate carrot and onion. Put in a large pan with remaining ingredients except lobster. Bring to the boil, then lower heat and simmer, uncovered, for 25 minutes.

Leave to cool, then strain. Return to rinsed out pan. Immerse lobster in court bouillon, heat gently to boiling point, then lower the heat and cover with a lid. Simmer 15 minutes for lobsters up to 1 lb, 20 minutes up to 2 lb. The lobster is ready when the shell turns bright red. Drain and leave to cool, then refrigerate until required.

This is reputed to be the most humane way to kill a lobster and at the same time ensure moist, tender flesh.

Cold appetizers

Crayfish

Crayfish are delicious, but unfortunately rare in many parts of the world. If you are lucky enough to get some, cook them simply – the way the Scandinavians do – in a rich cream and wine sauce that makes a kind of crayfish soup.

crayfish
about 1⅓ cups of dry white wine
few sprigs of fennel or dill
1⅓ cups heavy cream
salt and pepper

To serve
hot French bread

Put the crayfish in a large pan and pour over enough wine to cover. Add the fennel or dill, then pour in the cream.

Bring to the boil, lower the heat and cover with a lid. Simmer 7 – 8 minutes until the crayfish are bright pink.

Discard fennel or dill. Season to taste with salt and pepper. Chill. Spoon crayfish and sauce into soup bowls and serve with hot French or garlic bread. This is also delicious served hot.

Crayfish, a rare delight!

Crab Cocktail

1 small lettuce heart
salt and pepper
½ cucumber
watercress
¾ cup shredded white
 and brown crabmeat, mixed
juice of ½ lemon

To garnish
chopped parsley

Separate lettuce leaves and use to line base of serving bowl or glasses. Sprinkle with salt and pepper. Chop half of the cucumber finely and slice remaining half thinly. Chop watercress finely.

Mix chopped cucumber, watercress and crab together. Add salt and pepper to taste. Spoon onto lettuce leaves and sprinkle with lemon juice. Cut each slice of cucumber through to the center, form into spiral shapes and use to garnish. Sprinkle with parsley and serve with Green Sauce.

Green Sauce

1 small bunch of fresh spinach, chives,
 parsley or basil
¾ cup basic mayonnaise
2 tsp fresh orange juice
salt and pepper

Put the spinach or herbs in a pan, cover with water and boil for 2–3 minutes. Strain and leave to cool. Chop finely, then strain through a sieve or foodmill.

Stir mayonnaise into strained mixture with orange juice and salt and pepper to taste. Mix well to combine, then transfer to a serving bowl or jug. Keep in a cool place until ready to serve.

HOW TO CLEAN AND PREPARE A CRAB

Crabs are usually sold ready cooked, but if you are lucky enough to find fresh crabs alive, boil them gently in salted water or a court bouillon, allowing 15 minutes per pound. Then dress or prepare as shown.

Dressed crab served in the shell.

1. Rinse the crab under cold water and dry with absorbent paper. The first step to prepare the crab is to break or twist off all the claws.

2. Then grip the shell firmly and pull the crab's body away from the shell.

3. There are several parts which are inedible or poisonous and therefore must be removed. First, discard the poisonous gray 'fingers' or lungs.

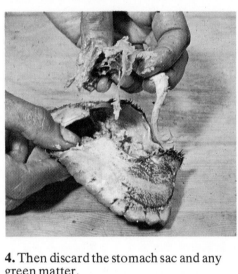

4. Then discard the stomach sac and any green matter.

5. In the foreground are pictured all the parts of the crab that are to be thrown away. The body being held behind contains the white meat which should be removed with the help of a skewer. Crack the large claws with a hammer or nutcrackers, then remove all white meat with a skewer. (If preferred, the large claws can be left whole and cracked at the table.)

To serve dressed crab in the shell

Wash and dry shell thoroughly. Season both white and dark meats liberally with salt and pepper. Add lemon juice to taste. Spoon white and dark meat into shell, keeping them separate.

Arrange shell on serving platter and decorate with sieved hardcooked eggs and finely chopped parsley. Arrange small claws around shell. If large claws were left whole, arrange these around shell also. Serve with basic mayonnaise, and provide nutcrackers for guests to extract white meat from large claws if left whole.

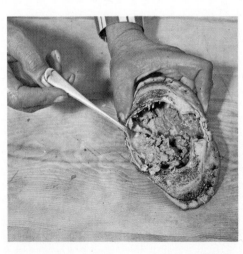

6. Scoop out the dark meat from the main shell. Shred the white and dark meat.

Serve freshly caught shrimps hot or cold with French bread.

Shrimps with Lemon and Fennel

If you are lucky enough to obtain freshly caught shrimps, then this is one of the simplest and best ways to serve them. Leave guests to remove shells themselves as this makes the meal fun.

shrimps
⅔ cup dry white wine
water
thinly pared rind of 1 lemon
few sticks fresh fennel
2 bay leaves
salt
few black peppercorns

Wash the shrimps thoroughly under cold running water, then put in a pan with the wine and enough water to cover. Add the remaining ingredients.

Bring to the boil, then lower the heat. Half cover with a lid and simmer for 4–10 minutes until the shrimps turn brown. The length of time this takes will vary according to size and number of shrimps and the length of time since they were caught.

Drain. Cool, and serve with lemon wedges and French bread and butter. This is also delicious hot.

Prawn and Cucumber Brioche

For brioche
2 cakes compressed yeast
¼ cup sugar
1⅓ cups milk at blood heat
3¾ cups flour
¼ tsp salt
1 tsp baking powder
¼ cup butter or margarine
3 eggs

For filling
1 cucumber
1 cup shelled prawns
⅔ cup basic mayonnaise
juice of ½ orange
⅔ cup heavy cream
3–4 drops Tabasco sauce
salt and pepper

For garnish
¼ cup shelled prawns

Put the yeast and sugar in a large warmed bowl and work together with the back of a wooden spoon until a liquid is formed. Stir

Prawn and Cucumber Brioche.

in the milk gradually. Sift 1 cup of flour with the salt and beat into the yeast and milk mixture a little at a time until smooth.

Cover with a damp cloth and leave to prove in a warm place for about 30 minutes or until doubled in bulk. Meanwhile, brush the inside of a 5 cup fluted brioche pan liberally with oil and set aside. Set the oven at 400°F. Sift remaining flour and the baking powder into a large bowl, then rub in the butter or margarine with the fingertips until evenly distributed. Make a well in the center.

When the yeast mixture has doubled in bulk, pour into the well in the center of the flour. Stir with a wooden spoon, gradually incorporating the flour into the yeast mixture. When half the flour is incorporated, break in the eggs one at a time and stir to incorporate with more flour. Continue stirring gently until the mixture is thoroughly blended.

Pour the mixture into the prepared brioche pan and bake in preset oven for 30 minutes until the brioche is well risen and golden brown. Turn out onto a wire rack

and leave to cool.

Meanwhile, prepare the filling. Peel and dice cucumber. Roughly chop prawns. Mix all the filling ingredients together, adding salt and pepper to taste.

When the brioche is cold, cut the lid from the top and carefully hollow out the center of the brioche, retaining the base and leaving about ¼ inch of bread around the sides.

Turn the brioche onto a serving platter. Spoon the prepared filling into the hollow in the center of the brioche and replace the lid. Garnish with prawns and serve.

HOW TO MAKE GRAVLAX

This is the traditional Swedish method of marinating fresh salmon. You should allow a thin slice from the middle cut for each person.

1. Put 1 slice of salmon flat on a board and sprinkle with sea salt.

2. Cover with sprigs of fresh dill (or fennel if no dill is available).

3. Put another slice of salmon on top. Continue with these layers until all the slices of salmon are used.

4. Cover with a piece of waxed paper.

Serve with traditional mustard sauce and brown bread and butter. Garnish with lemon wedges.

5. Put a board on top of the paper and put heavy weights on top. Leave to marinate in the refrigerator for 48 hours, then wash the salmon slices under cold running water and wipe dry.

Prawns served in a tasty fish aspic.

Prawns in a Mold

Shrimps may be substituted for the prawns.

caramel food coloring
cochineal food coloring
3¾ cups unset basic fish aspic
¾ cup shelled and veined prawns

For garnish
watercress
¼–½ cup unshelled prawns

Dip a skewer into the caramel food coloring and shake a few drops over the aspic. Repeat with the cochineal coloring. Stir

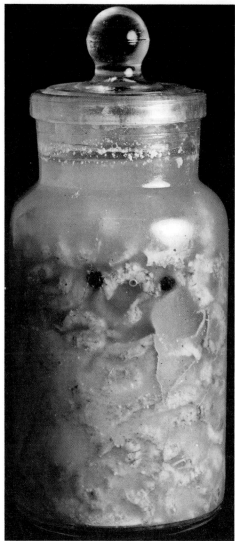

Potted Shrimps.

thoroughly until the colors are evenly mixed.

Pour the aspic into a wetted 5 cup ring mold and chill in the refrigerator until just beginning to set. Push the prawns into the aspic jelly, using your fingers to space them evenly apart. Return mold to the refrigerator and chill until set, preferably overnight.

Turn the mold out onto a serving platter. Arrange the watercress in the center and garnish around the mold with the unshelled prawns. Serve with thinly sliced brown bread and butter.

Potted Shrimps
or Prawns

1¼ cups butter
2 small bay leaves
4 black peppercorns
dash of powdered mace
3 cups shelled shrimps
  or 2 cups shelled prawns

Put the butter in a pan and heat very gently until melted. Do not let the butter become brown. When the bubbling has stopped, remove pan from heat.

Leave to stand 2–3 minutes, then pour off the clear liquid that has risen to the surface, leaving the sediment behind.

Crumble the bay leaves until very fine. Crush the peppercorns in a mortar with a pestle. Sprinkle bay leaves, peppercorns and mace into clarified butter.

Put the shrimps or prawns into a glass jar or earthenware container and pour in the clarified butter. Leave until set, then chill in the refrigerator. Serve with triangles of hot toast, lemon wedges and freshly ground black pepper.

HOW TO BONE HERRINGS

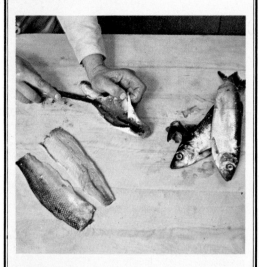

1. Wash thoroughly and remove scales by scraping with a knife. Remove the heads and tails, then split down the underside.

2. Open the herring out as flat as possible.

3. Remove the backbone carefully, starting at the head and slipping your finger or a knife under it as you pull. Then remove all the side bones and wash thoroughly under cold running water and dry thoroughly.

Herrings stored in a glass jar.

Fish Aspic

Basic Recipe

3¾ cups basic fish stock
1 egg white
1 tbsp wine vinegar
1¼ cups dry white wine or apple cider
2 egg shells
3 packets (3 tbsp) powdered gelatin

Put the stock, egg white, wine vinegar and wine or apple cider in a scrupulously clean large saucepan. Crush the egg shells and add to the pan. Sprinkle the gelatin over the surface. Heat gently to simmering point over a low heat, beating constantly to make a thick froth rise to the surface.

As soon as the liquid starts to simmer, stop beating and move the pan to the side of the heat so that only half of the pan is over the heat. Simmer very gently for 15 minutes, turning the pan around every 5 minutes so that a different part is over the heat.

Line a colander or sieve with several layers of scrupulously clean muslin and place over a clean mixing bowl. Ladle the liquid very gently into the lined colander or sieve and allow to strain through. Leave until cold, then chill in the refrigerator before use.

Marinated Sea Herrings

6 sea herrings
2 medium onions
6 strips of lemon peel
6 small bay leaves
2 tsp peppercorns

For marinade
¾ cup red wine vinegar
¾ cup water

Clean and bone herrings as shown.

Cut each herring into 2 fillets. Roll up each fillet, starting from the tail end. Secure with wooden cocktail picks.

Peel the onions and slice into fine rings. Pack the herrings into a glass jar, alternating them with rings of onion, strips of lemon peel, bay leaves and peppercorns.

Put the wine vinegar and water in a pan and heat gently, but do not allow to boil. When quite hot, pour into the jar.

Cover with a lid. Leave to cool, then chill in the refrigerator for 48 hours. Serve with hot crusty French bread and butter.

Individual Mousse of Herring Roes

½ lb soft herring roes
1 inch thick slice of crustless white bread
2–3 tbsp dry white wine or water
1 tsp anchovy flavoring
⅔ cup light cream
⅔ cup creamy milk
salt and pepper
1 package gelatin
4 tbsp water
3 egg whites

For garnish
8 stuffed olives
1 lettuce heart
tomatoes

Put the herring roes in the top of a steamer or double boiler, cover with a lid and steam for 7–10 minutes until tender.

Meanwhile, moisten the bread with wine or water. Put in a bowl with the steamed roes, anchovy flavoring, cream and milk and stir well to combine. Purée in an electric blender or strain through a sieve until smooth. Season to taste with salt and pepper.

Sprinkle the gelatin over the water in a small heatproof bowl and leave until spongy. Stand the bowl in a pan of gently simmering water until gelatin has dissolved, then stir into the roe mixture.

Beat the egg whites until stiff, then fold into the roe mixture until evenly mixed. Spoon into 8 oiled individual soufflé or ramekin dishes and chill in the refrigerator until set.

Unmold each mousse onto a serving platter and top each one with a stuffed olive. Garnish the platter with lettuce leaves and tomatoes. Serve with rolls of thinly sliced brown bread and butter.

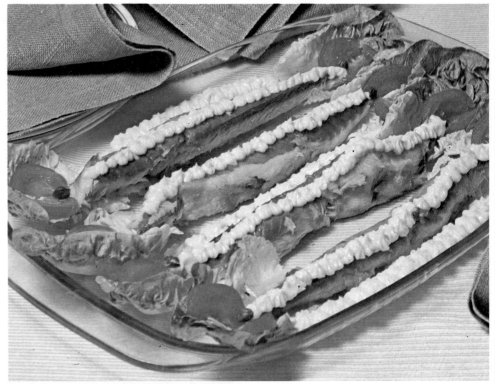
Smoked mackerel garnished with mayonnaise.

Individual Mousse of Herring Roes.

Mackerel Mayonnaise

1 large smoked mackerel
juice of 1 lemon
freshly ground black pepper
⅔ cup basic mayonnaise

To garnish
1 lettuce heart
2 ripe tomatoes
8 capers

Cut along the backbone of the mackerel, then carefully remove skin with the point of a sharp knife. Lift out the exposed flesh by easing the blade of knife between the bones and the flesh above it.

Turn over the fish and repeat this process on the other side. Cut each piece of fish lengthwise in two. Sprinkle with lemon juice and plenty of black pepper.

Arrange the pièces of fish on a serving platter. Pipe mayonnaise decoratively on top of fish. Garnish platter with lettuce leaves, quartered tomatoes and capers. Chill in the refrigerator until serving time.

Cold appetizers

Sardine Salad

3 × 4⅜ cans of sardines in oil
1–2 tsp wine vinegar
pepper
6 hardcooked eggs
few sprigs of fresh parsley
3 lemons
basic French dressing made
    with 1¼ cups of oil

Drain 6 sardines, remove the tails and
bones and mash the sardines with wine
vinegar and pepper to taste. Arrange near
the center of an oval serving platter.

Drain the remaining sardines and
arrange in a fan shape on the platter.
Separate the whites and yolks of the eggs
and chop finely, keeping whites and yolks
separate.

Arrange the whites and yolks in
separate sections on the platter around the
sardines. Put a border of parsley heads
along the outside edge of the whole sardines. Cut the lemons into decorative
slices, using a canelle knife if you have
one, and use to garnish the dish, adding
thin strips of lemon peel around the edge.
Serve with French dressing.

Herrings Vinaigrette

½ lb kippered herring fillets
1 clove of garlic
8 tbsp corn or vegetable oil
3 tbsp wine vinegar
1 tsp crushed black peppercorns

To finish
1 large Spanish onion
1 tbsp capers
few sprigs of parsley
4 lemon wedges

Remove skin and any large bones from
kippered herrings and discard. Put
kippered herrings in a shallow dish. Peel
and crush the garlic and stir into the oil
with the vinegar and pepper. Beat well to
mix. Pour over the kippered herrings and
leave to marinate in the refrigerator overnight, spooning over the dressing from
time to time.

Arrange kippered herrings in a serving
dish and spoon over the dressing. Peel the
onion, slice into fine rings and use to garnish the kippered herrings with drained
capers and sprigs of parsley. Serve with
lemon wedges and French bread.

Sardine Salad.

Crab Dip

1 can (8 oz) water chestnuts
1 tbsp fresh ginger root
2 cups (1 lb) crabmeat
2 tbsp soy sauce
¼ cup basic mayonnaise

For garnish
6–8 crab claws

For serving
bread sticks
celery sticks

Drain and chop the water chestnuts. Chop
the fresh ginger root. Shred the crabmeat.
Mix all the ingredients until well combined, then cover and chill until serving
time. Garnish with the crab claws, if liked,
and serve with bread sticks and celery
sticks for dipping.

Avocado Prawn

2 ripe avocados
juice of 1 lemon
⅜ cup water
1½ cups shelled prawns
4 rounded tbsp basic mayonnaise
4 drops of Tabasco sauce
1 tsp paprika
salt and pepper
1 lettuce heart

Peel the avocados, then cut in half
lengthwise, using a silver knife. Remove
seeds. Slice the flesh thinly without
separating the slices from each other. Put
in a single layer in a shallow dish.

Mix lemon juice and water together and
pour over the avocados. Leave to steep for
10 minutes, spooning the dressing over
the avocados occasionally.

Put the prawns in a bowl, then add the
mayonnaise, Tabasco and paprika with
salt and pepper to taste. Mix well to
combine.

Shred the lettuce heart and arrange in the bottom of 4 individual serving glasses or bowls. Spoon the prawn mixture over the shredded lettuce, dividing it equally amongst the 4 glasses.

Arrange 1 sliced avocado half in each glass, then chill in the refrigerator. Serve with thinly sliced white or brown bread and butter.

Avocado and Walnut Dip

½ green pepper
1 small onion
1 tbsp walnuts
2 avocados
½ cup sour cream
freshly ground black pepper
squeeze of lemon juice

Blanch the green pepper and then plunge in cold water and chop finely. Grate the onion finely. Chop the walnuts.

Cut the avocados in half, remove seeds, and scoop out the flesh. Mix with a fork, adding the sour cream, black pepper, grated onion and lemon juice. Then add the green pepper and the walnuts. Chill before serving.

Serve with a variety of 'dippers' such as savory crackers, chips, French bread, and sticks of celery and carrot.

Mustard Sauce

2 tbsp prepared hot mustard
1 tbsp sugar
1 egg yolk
2 tbsp vinegar
½ cup oil
2 tbsp chopped dill
salt and pepper

Mix the mustard, sugar, egg yolk and vinegar and beat well. Beat in the oil a little at a time until the mixture thickens slightly. Then beat in the remaining oil in a steady stream. Add the dill and season to taste – the sauce should be hot but not fiery.

Mussels with Cream

3 dozen fresh mussels
juice of 1 lemon
⅔ cup light cream
salt and pepper

To finish
finely chopped parsley

Scrub mussels thoroughly under cold running water. Discard beards and any mussels that are open. Soak cleaned mussels for 1 hour in cold water, then drain and place in the top of a steamer. Cover with a lid and steam over high heat for 5 to 10 minutes until the mussels open.

Discard any that are still closed. Scrape mussels from their shells and arrange in a serving dish. Sprinkle over the lemon juice. Season the cream with salt and pepper to taste and pour over the mussels in the dish. Chill in the refrigerator for 2 hours, then sprinkle with parsley just before serving. Allow about 9 mussels per person.

Mushrooms in Sour Cream

1 lb fresh button mushrooms
juice of ¼ lemon
⅔ cup sour cream
salt and pepper

To finish
paprika

Wipe the mushrooms clean with a damp cloth, but do not peel. Slice thinly into a bowl and sprinkle with lemon juice to prevent discoloration. Add the sour cream with salt and pepper to taste and mix gently until the mushrooms are coated in the cream.

Transfer to a serving dish, sprinkle with paprika to taste and chill in the refrigerator until serving time. Serve with French bread.

Mussels with Cream and Mushrooms in Sour Cream.

Cold appetizers

Serving ideas for avocado pears.

Avocado Vinaigrette

2 avocados
½ lemon
basic French dressing made with
    1⅓ cups oil

Cut the avocados in half lengthwise, using a silver knife. Remove seeds. Rub the exposed flesh with the cut surface of a lemon to prevent discoloration. Arrange 1 avocado half on each individual serving plate. Pour French dressing over avocados and serve as soon as possible.

As an alternative, substitute Madeira for the French dressing. Cut the avocados in half as above, then score the flesh in diagonal lines. Arrange on individual plates, pour 1–2 tbsp Madeira into each avocado half and leave to steep for 1–2 minutes before serving.

Avocado with Crab

4–6 rounded tbsp basic mayonnaise
4 drops of Tabasco sauce
½ tsp paprika
scant 1 tsp lemon juice
salt and pepper
scant ¾ cup fresh or frozen
    crabmeat
2 avocados
½ lemon

Blend 4 tbsp mayonnaise thoroughly with the Tabasco, paprika and lemon juice and season to taste with salt and pepper. Mix the white and dark crabmeat and fold into the mayonnaise. Set aside.

Cut the avocados, remove the seeds and rub with lemon to avoid discoloration. Spoon the prepared crabmeat mixture into the avocados. If liked, pipe rosettes of remaining mayonnaise around the edge of each avocado half. Serve as soon as possible.

If no crabmeat is available, substitute 1 cup shelled and veined prawns or shrimps for the crabmeat.

HOW TO MAKE CUCUMBER TUBS

Cucumber Tubs

1 large cucumber
salt
2 rounded tbsp basic mayonnaise
¼ tsp cayenne pepper
¾ cup shelled and veined prawns
    or shrimps

To finish
4–5 fried bread croûtons
4–5 strips of tomato
1 large bunch parsley

Cut both ends off the cucumber and discard, then cut cucumber into 4 or 5 equal portions. Cut a very thin slice off each one and set aside.

Decorate and hollow out each portion as shown. Sprinkle with salt; leave to drain in a colander or sieve for 30 minutes, then wipe the insides dry with absorbent paper.

Blend the mayonnaise with cayenne pepper. Chop the prawns or shrimps roughly, setting aside 4–5 whole ones for decoration. Fold into the mayonnaise.

Arrange croûtons on a serving dish or platter. Place one cucumber portion on each, then carefully spoon in the mayonnaise mixture. Garnish the top of each portion with reserved cucumber slices and whole prawns or shrimps and decorate with strips of tomato. Garnish with parsley and chill until serving time.

1. To give a striped effect, cut fine strips from top to bottom of each portion, using a sharp knife.

2. Using a serrated knife, cut around the inside flesh and carefully hollow out each portion.

Cucumber Tubs.

Cold appetizers

Aspic

Basic Recipe ⭐

2 pt (8 cups) homemade
    jellied stock
salt and pepper
2 egg whites
⅓ cup ground beef
2 tsp finely chopped fresh tarragon,
    or 1 tsp dried tarragon
⅔ cup Madeira, port or sherry

It is essential to have well flavored jellied stock in order to make good aspic. Use calf's feet, veal knuckles, marrow bones and pork rind for making the stock and simmer it for a long time so that it will be rich and well reduced.

Chill the stock in the refrigerator, then remove all traces of grease that have risen to the surface. Season stock with salt and pepper to taste.

Put 1 cup of stock in a scrupulously clean mixing bowl. Add the egg whites, ground beef and tarragon and beat with a whisk. Strain remaining stock into a scrupulously clean saucepan and bring to the boil. Remove from heat and pour into bowl in a steady stream, beating constantly.

Return mixture to pan and heat gently to simmering point, stirring constantly. As soon as the liquid starts to simmer, stop stirring and move the pan to the side of the heat so that only half of the pan is over the heat. Simmer the liquid for 15 minutes, turning the pan around every 5 minutes so that a different part of the pan is over the heat.

Line a colander or sieve with several layers of scrupulously clean muslin and place over a clean mixing bowl. Ladle the stock very gently into the lined colander or sieve and allow to strain through. When all the aspic has strained through, stir in the Madeira, port or sherry. Leave until cold, then chill in the refrigerator until set. If unset aspic is required for a recipe, then simply heat aspic jelly gently and it will become liquid.

If a very firm aspic is required, sprinkle 1 tsp powdered gelatin over a little stock in a small heatproof bowl. Stand bowl in a pan of gently simmering water, heat gently to dissolve. Stir into unset aspic. Chill in the refrigerator before use.

Vegetables in Aspic

3¾ cups unset basic aspic
few sprigs of parsley, tarragon
    or winter savory
4 small zucchini
¼ cucumber
½ red pimento
2 hardcooked eggs
⅔ cup heavy cream
⅔ cup basic mayonnaise
1 package gelatin
3 tbsp water
salt and pepper

To garnish
1–2 lettuce hearts

Use a large mold or several individual ones. Allow the aspic to become syrupy, then use to coat the base and sides of a wetted 5 cup mold or 8 wetted individual molds. Chill in the refrigerator until set. Cover with a second coating of aspic, then place a small sprig of parsley, tarragon or savory in the center of the mold(s). Cover with a little more aspic to seal the herbs, then chill in the refrigerator until set.

Meanwhile, peel the zucchini and dice finely. Place in the top of a steamer and steam for about 7 minutes until tender. Leave to cool. Peel the cucumber and grate coarsely into a bowl. Remove the pith and seeds from the pimento, dice finely and mix with the cucumber. Chop the hardcooked eggs roughly and stir into the vegetable mixture with the cooled zucchini.

Whip the cream until thick, then mix into the mayonnaise until thoroughly combined. Sprinkle the gelatin over the water in a small heatproof bowl and leave until spongy. Stand the bowl in a pan of gently simmering water until gelatin has dissolved, then remove from the heat and leave to cool slightly.

Stir the liquid gelatin into the cream and mayonnaise mixture, then fold into the mixed vegetables and eggs. Stir to combine and season to taste with salt and pepper.

Spoon the vegetable mixture into the mold(s), leaving room for another layer of aspic. Chill until set. Coat with a thin layer of aspic to seal. Refrigerate. Unmold, garnish with lettuce.

HOW TO PREPARE GLOBE

Artichokes
with French Dressing

4 artichokes
½ lemon
basic French dressing made
    with 1⅓ cups oil

Cut the stalks off the artichokes, then remove any tough or damaged outer leaves. Cut off the top peaks of the petals. Wash thoroughly under cold running water, drain. Rub cut surfaces with lemon.

Put artichokes in the top of a steamer or in a pan of boiling salted water and steam or boil young ones for 25 minutes, older ones for 30–40 minutes, depending on age. The artichokes are ready when an outer leaf can be pulled out easily. Remove from steamer or pan, turn upside down to drain and leave to cool.

Prepare artichokes as shown. Replace the caps upside down in the center of the artichokes, then arrange on individual serving plates. Pour French dressing into the center of each artichoke.

1. Pull the artichokes open gently with the fingers to expose the centers.

2. Continue until you expose the peaked cap which is slightly paler in color.

ARTICHOKES

The prepared globe artichokes ready for filling.

3. Pull out the peaked cap from the center by twisting slowly.

4. Set the cap aside, as this is edible. The inedible hairy choke is now exposed.

5. Using your fingers or a teaspoon, scrape out the hairy choke and discard.

A dip is perfect for informal parties.

Bagna Cauda

Bagna Cauda is a simple Italian idea of dipping raw vegetables into hot oil flavored with anchovies, garlic and black pepper. Guests help themselves, therefore it is particularly suitable for informal buffet parties.

2 × 2 oz cans of anchovy fillets in oil
milk
6 cloves of garlic
1⅓ cups olive oil
¼ tsp crushed black peppercorns

To serve
raw salad vegetables (carrot, celery, French endive, radish, scallions, etc.)

Drain the anchovies and place in a bowl. Cover with milk and leave to soak for at least 30 minutes. Drain and pat dry with absorbent paper, then chop finely.

Peel the cloves of garlic and cut into fine slivers. Pour the oil into a heavy based pan and heat gently on the stove. When hot, stir in the anchovies, garlic and crushed peppercorns and transfer pan to a fondue stand over a spirit flame. Keep the oil hot while guests dip in the vegetables.

Crudités

Crudités, or raw vegetable salad, is one of the simplest of starters to prepare and is suitable for informal occasions such as barbecues. Your choice of vegetables will obviously be determined by the season and, although summer is the best time of year for preparing this kind of appetizer, interesting salads can be made with imaginative use of winter vegetables such as cauliflower, carrots and cabbage. For a slimmer's version, substitute lemon juice or wine vinegar for the mayonnaise and French dressing suggested.

cabbage (red and hard white)
carrot
cauliflower
celeriac or celery root
celery
French endive
cucumber
fennel
leek
mushroom
pimento (pepper)
radish

scallions
tomato
basic mayonnaise and/or basic French dressing

Choose a variety of vegetables from the ones listed, depending on availability. Prepare for eating raw, either by washing under cold running water or by trimming, scraping and wiping clean.

Arrange chosen vegetables in a serving dish or basket and set in the center of table. Provide guests with sharp knives, graters, chopping boards, etc. and let them help themselves. Serve bowls or jugs of mayonnaise and/or French dressing separately as dips. Guests can then help themselves.

An unusual edible centerpiece to decorate your table.

Cold appetizers

Anchovy and Egg Mousse

2 × 2 oz cans of anchovy fillets in oil
milk
⅓ cup sweet butter
1–2 tsp lemon juice
6 hardcooked eggs
⅓ cup heavy cream
pepper

To garnish
paprika
basic anchovy butter (optional)

Drain the anchovies and place in a bowl. Cover with milk and leave to soak for at least 30 minutes.

Meanwhile, cream the butter with an electric or rotary beater until light and fluffy.

Drain the anchovies and pat dry with absorbent paper. Pound to a paste in a mortar with a pestle with the lemon juice. Work the anchovy paste into the creamed butter a little at a time until smooth and evenly colored. Work the hardcooked eggs through a fine sieve and beat into the anchovy mixture a little at a time. Whip the cream until thick and fold into the mixture, adding plenty of pepper.

Form the mousse into the shape of a small cake on a serving platter. Make ridges on the surface of the mousse with the back of a fork. Sprinkle with a little paprika and decorate with a piped rosette of anchovy butter, if liked.

Chill in the refrigerator for several hours, then serve with hot crusty bread and sweet butter.

If you wish to pipe a trellis of leaves over the mousse for decoration this can easily be done by coloring whipped butter with a few drops of green food coloring and piping this onto the mousse.

Anchovy and Egg Mousse with some garnishing suggestions.

Stuffed Peppers

5–6 medium green peppers
6 eggs
2 tbsp tomato paste
1 tsp paprika
6 tbsp chilled butter or margarine
1 small onion
salt and pepper
2–4 boiled new potatoes
1 cooked carrot
⅓ cup cooked peas

To serve
hot garlic or French bread

Cut the tops off the peppers and reserve. Scoop out the pith and pips using a grapefruit knife. Wash thoroughly under cold running water, then pat dry with absorbent paper. Set aside.

Beat the eggs in a bowl with the tomato paste and paprika. Grate 2 tbsp butter or margarine into the egg mixture.

Peel the onion and chop very finely. Melt the remaining butter or margarine in a pan, add the onion and fry gently until soft and golden. Pour in the egg mixture and scramble over low heat, stirring constantly. Season to taste with salt and pepper. Leave to cool.

For formal gatherings, serve Stuffed Apricots.

Dice the potatoes and carrot very finely, then add to the scrambled eggs with the peas. Stir well to mix. Taste for seasoning. Spoon the mixture into the prepared peppers and replace tops. Chill in the refrigerator until serving time.

Arrange on serving dish and garnish with lettuce leaves or some chopped vegetables. Serve with hot garlic or French bread.

Stuffed Apricots

½ lb fresh apricots
½ an 8 oz package cream cheese
1 tbsp anchovy flavoring
1–2 tbsp basic mayonnaise
pink food coloring
pepper

To serve
few sprigs of curly endive

Halve the apricots and remove stones. Set aside.

Beat the cream cheese until soft. Stir in the anchovy flavoring and enough mayonnaise to make a consistency for piping. Dip a skewer into the pink food coloring, then shake into the cream cheese mixture. Stir well to mix, adding more food coloring if necessary until the mixture is pale pink. Add pepper to taste.

Spoon the mixture into a pastry bag fitted with a star nozzle and pipe into the halved apricots. Arrange the curly endive on a serving platter and place the apricots on top. Chill in the refrigerator until serving time.

Cold appetizers

Melon and Orange Cocktail

1 large honeydew melon
4 large oranges
2 tsp medium or dry sherry
¼ tsp ginger

For sweet orange sauce
juice of 4 oranges
1 tbsp light brown sugar
½–1 tsp cinnamon

Cut a slice off the base of the melon so that it will stand upright. Cut melon into a basket shape with a handle by removing 2 sections from the top, leaving a thin strip of skin in the center. Scoop out the flesh with a melon baller or sharp knife, discarding all seeds. Snip the edges of the melon with scissors to make a zigzag pattern. Set aside.

Skin the oranges and divide into segments. Remove all pith and seeds. Put in a bowl with the melon flesh, sprinkle with the sherry and ginger and leave to marinate for approximately 15 minutes, stirring occasionally.

Meanwhile, make the sauce. Put the orange juice and sugar in a pan and heat gently until the sugar has dissolved. Increase the heat and boil rapidly for 1–2 minutes, then remove from the heat and leave to cool.

Arrange the melon basket and sections in serving dishes. Spoon in the marinated melon and orange, using any remaining pieces to garnish the dishes. Pour the cooled sauce into a dish or jug and sprinkle with the cinnamon. Keep in a cool place until serving time. Serve the sauce separately for guests to spoon over cocktails.

Green Ice Grapefruit

2 grapefruit
2 tbsp sugar
2 tbsp dry vermouth or sherry
2 maraschino cherries (optional)

For crushed ice
water
green food coloring

Cut a slice off the base of each grapefruit so that they will stand upright on the crushed ice. Cut off the tops and snip the top edge of the skin with scissors to make a zigzag pattern.

Some serving suggestions for Melon and Orange Cocktail.

Scoop out the flesh with a grapefruit knife. Discard pips, pith and central core. Cut the flesh into bite sized pieces. Put flesh in a bowl and sprinkle with the sugar and vermouth or sherry. Stir gently to combine. Spoon into hollowed out grapefruits and stand in individual glass serving dishes on bowls of crushed ice. Top each grapefruit with a maraschino cherry, if liked. Serve immediately.

To make crushed ice, make ice cubes with water in the usual way, adding 1 or 2 drops of green food coloring and stirring well. When the cubes are frozen solid, wrap in paper and crush with a hammer or kitchen mallet.

Grapefruit and Crab Cups for a dinner party starter.

Grapefruit and Crab Cups

2 medium grapefruit
½ cup shredded white crabmeat
¼ cucumber
2 tbsp basic mayonnaise
1 tbsp cultured sour cream or plain
    unsweetened yogurt
cayenne pepper, to taste
salt

To garnish
2 bay leaves (optional)
cucumber slices
tomatoes
lettuce leaves

Cut a thin slice off the base of each grapefruit so that they will stand upright on platter. Cut off the tops and reserve for lids.

Snip the top edge of the skin with scissors to make a zigzag pattern, then scoop out all the flesh, seeds and pith from inside the grapefruit. Discard seeds, pith and central core. Cut the flesh into bite sized pieces.

Flake the crabmeat and dice the cucumber finely. Mix with the grapefruit flesh. Fold in the mayonnaise and sour cream or yogurt. Add a pinch of cayenne pepper and salt to taste. Stir gently until evenly mixed.

Spoon the crab mixture into the prepared grapefruit cases and replace lids, with bay leaves pressed into them, if liked. Place on a serving platter and garnish with cucumber, tomato and lettuce.

Green Ice Grapefruit.

Cold appetizers

Spiced Cream Cheese with Melon

8 oz package cream cheese
1–2 tbsp top of the milk
ginger, to taste
salt
4 round slices of honeydew melon

To garnish
4 large black olives
8 small lettuce leaves
paprika

Beat the cream cheese with the top of the milk until soft. Add about 1 tsp of ginger, and salt to taste, then beat again to distribute evenly. Set aside.

Discard the seeds from the center of the melon and cut away the skin. If you wish to use the skins to make decorative handles, then cut these to shape and set aside. Stamp the edges of the slices with a fluted cookie cutter if liked, or cut in a decorative pattern with a sharp pointed knife. Arrange on individual serving plates.

Divide the cream cheese mixture into 4 equal portions and mound into dome shapes in the center of melon slices, smoothing the cheese carefully with a small palette knife.

Pit the olives and cut the flesh into thin strips. Garnish each cream cheese dome with a few strips of olive. Press 2 lettuce leaves into the base of each dome, 1 on each side, then dust with a little paprika. Place melon skin handles over the salads, if using. Refrigerate until serving time.

Spiced Cream Cheese with Melon.

Avocado with Strawberries and Cream Cheese

This salad makes a perfect appetizer for a summer meal served outside.

8 oz package cream cheese
¼ cup roasted filberts
salt and pepper
3 cups small strawberries
2 ripe avocados
juice of 1 lemon
¾ cup water
2–3 tbsp sugar

To serve
fresh orange juice

Beat the cream cheese until soft. Chop the filberts very finely or grind them in a foodmill or electric grinder. Beat into the cream cheese until evenly mixed and season to taste with salt and pepper. Pipe or mound mixture in the center of a serving dish. Chill in the refrigerator.

Wash and clean the strawberries and set aside. Peel the avocados, then cut in half lengthwise, using a silver knife. Remove seeds. Cut 1 avocado into thin slices. Mix lemon juice and water together and pour over the avocados to prevent discoloration.

Assemble halved avocados and strawberries around cream cheese on serving dish, then arrange sliced avocados around edge of dish to make an attractive pattern. Sprinkle strawberries with sugar to taste. Serve immediately with fresh orange juice separately for guests to pour over their salads.

Stuffed Apples with a simple garnish of apple leaves.

Stuffed Apples

6 red eating apples
juice of 1 lemon
3 stalks of celery
¼ cup lean boiled ham, finely chopped
¼ cup walnut halves
3 tbsp basic mayonnaise
salt and pepper

To serve
1 lettuce heart
6 freshly picked apple leaves
¾ cup basic mayonnaise

Cut a slice off the bottom of each apple so that they will stand upright. Slice the tops off the apples, then carefully scoop out the apple flesh using a sharp teaspoon or knife. Discard apple cores and seeds, then grate flesh and immediately sprinkle with lemon juice to prevent discoloration.

Chop the celery, ham and walnuts very finely. Stir into the grated apple, then fold in the mayonnaise with salt and pepper to taste.

Spoon prepared filling into hollowed out apples. arrange 2 lettuce leaves in the base of each individual serving dish and place apple on top. Press 1 apple leaf into each filling to garnish and serve immediately with mayonnaise handed separately.

Hawaiian Orange Salad.

Hawaiian Orange Salad

2 large oranges
¼ cup Edam or Gouda cheese
1 celery heart
basic French dressing
　　made with ¼ cup oil
salt and pepper

To garnish
few sprigs parsley
few flower heads (optional)
1 small leaf lettuce

Cut a slice off the base of each orange so that they will stand upright. Cut through the orange skin and pith with a sharp pointed knife to make 6–8 petals in each orange. Do not cut right down to base or the petals will fall apart.

Remove flesh from inside oranges and discard pith and seeds. Skin the orange segments and slice flesh into bite sized pieces.

Remove rind from cheese and discard. Cut cheese into small cubes and mix with orange pieces. Dice the celery heart finely, reserving 1 stalk for the garnish.

Mix orange, cheese and celery with the French dressing and season to taste with salt and pepper. Spoon into the prepared orange skins. Shred the reserved celery stalk and use to garnish the tops of oranges.

Put oranges on individual serving plates and surround with sprigs of parsley. Arrange flower heads on plates if liked, and serve with a separate salad of leaf lettuce.

Cold appetizers

Russian Eggs.

Russian Eggs

4 thick slices of white bread
butter
4 hardcooked eggs
1 cup leftover cooked vegetables (peas,
carrots, potatoes, shelled beans, etc)
6 tbsp basic mayonnaise
salt and pepper
green coloring

To garnish
4 stuffed olives
watercress

Cut crusts from bread and discard. Stamp bread into rounds with a 4 inch diameter cookie cutter, then stamp a circle in the center of each round with a 1 inch cutter. Spread top and sides of bread rounds with butter and place on individual serving plates or dishes.

Cut each hardcooked egg into quarters without cutting right through to the base, and ease apart gently to form petals. Stand eggs upright in circles in bread rounds.

Chop or dice vegetables finely, if necessary, and combine with half the mayonnaise. Season to taste with salt and pepper. Spoon a little of this vegetable salad into the center of each egg. Spoon remaining salad around eggs to cover bread.

Add a few drops of green coloring to remaining mayonnaise and stir well to distribute the color evenly. Pipe in between quarters of egg. Place a stuffed olive on top of each egg and garnish with a little watercress. Chill in the refrigerator until serving time.

If preferred, the mixed vegetable salad for this appetizer may be bought ready prepared. It is available from most delicatessens and good supermarkets and is usually called Russian Salad.

Eggs and Pâté in Aspic.

Eggs and Pâté
in Aspic

1¼ cups unset basic aspic
¾ cup basic mayonnaise
6 hardcooked eggs
¼ lb liver pâté
1 tbsp heavy cream
1 tbsp medium or dry sherry
salt and pepper

To garnish
3 black olives
4 tbsp heavy cream

Pour ¼ cup aspic into a bowl and chill in the refrigerator until syrupy. Beat in the mayonnaise. Set over a bowl of ice cubes until beginning to thicken, then spoon over the eggs. Leave until set.

Meanwhile, beat the pâté with the cream and sherry until smooth. Season to taste with salt and pepper. Spoon or pipe into 6 individual soufflé or ramekin pots.

When the mayonnaise coating on the eggs has set, place eggs on top of pâté mixture. Pour remaining aspic into the pots, reserving 1–2 spoonfuls to set the decoration.

Halve black olives and remove pits. Place half a black olive on top of each egg, then spoon over the reserved aspic to set olive in position. Chill pots in the refrigerator until the aspic has set. Whip the cream until thick, then pipe small rosettes around each egg. Chill in the refrigerator until serving time.

Ham Mousse with some garnishing suggestions.

Ham Mousse

1 lb lean cooked ham
¾ cup thick basic velouté sauce
Tabasco sauce
1 package gelatin
4 tbsp ham or chicken stock
1¼ cups heavy cream
3 egg whites
salt and pepper

To garnish
slices of ham
parsley sprigs
1–2 tbsp prepared aspic

Grind the ham, then pound in a mortar, or pass through a sieve. Strain the velouté sauce through a sieve, then mix into the ham mixture. Season with salt and pepper and Tabasco, to taste.

Dissolve the gelatin in the stock. Whip the cream until it holds a loose shape. Whip the egg whites until stiff. Mix in the gelatin, and when the mixture begins to firm, carefully fold in the cream and then the egg whites, using a metal spoon. Fill into a deep soufflé dish and allow to set in the refrigerator. When set, unmold onto a serving dish. Roll up slices of ham and position around the mousse and add a sprig of parsley to each. Chop one slice of ham into small shapes and position on top. Pour over the aspic and allow to set in a cool place.

Rare Beef with Orange and Mustard Mayonnaise

12 thin slices of rare lean beef
2 cucumbers
7–8 small salad tomatoes

For orange garnish
3 oranges
4 rounded tbsp basic mayonnaise
1 tsp prepared French mustard
salt and pepper
1¼ cups mushrooms
1 bunch of watercress

Arrange the beef in a circle on a round serving platter. Slice the cucumber finely and arrange around the beef and in the center. Place whole tomatoes at regular intervals around the cucumber and 1 whole tomato in the center of the platter.

Divide each orange in two with a sharp pointed knife by cutting in a zigzag pattern right through to the center. Scoop out the flesh and strain through a sieve to extract the juice. Measure ¼ cup juice, put in a pan and boil to reduce until thick. Leave to cool, then stir into the mayonnaise with the mustard and salt and pepper to taste.

Wipe the mushrooms clean with a damp cloth, but do not peel. Chop or slice finely, then stir into the mayonnaise mixture.

Place the orange halves in between the tomatoes on the serving platter. Arrange a few sprigs of watercress in each orange, then top with 1–2 spoonfuls of the mayonnaise mixture.

Velouté Sauce

Basic Recipe

¼ cup butter or margarine
¾ cup flour
1 cup dry white wine
1¼ cups well flavored chicken stock
salt and pepper

Melt the butter or margarine in a pan. Stir in the flour with a wooden spoon and cook gently for 1–2 minutes until the mixture forms a soft ball, stirring constantly.

Stir in the wine gradually, beating vigorously all the time to obtain a smooth sauce. Add the stock and bring to the boil, stirring constantly.

Lower the heat and season to taste with salt and pepper. Simmer gently until the sauce thickens, stirring constantly.

This quantity makes 2½ cups of thick coating sauce. For a thinner pouring sauce use 3 tbsp butter or margarine and ¼ cup + 1 tbsp flour to 2½ cups wine and stock.

Cold appetizers

Cold Meat Platter

¼ lb sliced cooked tongue
¼ lb sliced garlic sausage
¼ lb sliced liver sausage
1 lettuce
1 hardcooked egg
basic French dressing
   made with ⅓ cup oil

For garnish
butter curls
2 large gherkins
2 radishes
few lemon wedges

Cut the tongue into 3 inch rounds with a fluted cookie cutter and arrange on a round serving platter. Skin the garlic sausage and arrange next to the tongue, overlapping slightly and reserving a few slices to decorate edge of platter. Repeat with liver sausage. Fold reserved slices of garlic and liver sausage into cornet shapes and arrange around edge of platter.

Shred the lettuce finely and place at opposite side of platter to folded cooked meats. Sieve the hardcooked egg and stir into the French dressing. Pour over the lettuce. Arrange butter curls around the lettuce.

Cut the gherkins into fan shapes by cutting into thin strips lengthwise, leaving a small amount of gherkin uncut at the base. Arrange on top of cooked meats, spreading out in fan shape. Top each fan with a cut radish. Place lemon wedges in cornets of garlic sausage.

The choice of cooked meats for this platter is a purely personal one and obviously can be varied according to taste and availability.

Ham Cornets

8 thin slices of lean boiled ham
¼ lb leftover cooked vegetables
   (peas, carrots, potatoes, broad beans, etc)
8 tbsp basic mayonnaise
salt and pepper

To garnish
1 large tomato
about ¼ cup ice cold butter
few sprigs of parsley

Fold each slice of ham into the shape of a cornet, using a cornet mold if available. Set aside with join underneath to prevent ham from unfolding.

Chop or dice vegetables finely, if necessary, and combine with 6 tbsp of the mayonnaise. Season to taste with salt and pepper. Spoon this vegetable salad into the ham cornets, dividing it equally amongst them. Arrange on a circular platter or a serving dish. Pipe remaining mayonnaise around edges of cornets. Chill in the refrigerator.

Meanwhile, cut tomato into 6 sections without cutting right through to base and ease apart gently to form petals. Cut butter into thin slices with a very sharp knife and stamp into small rounds with a fluted cookie cutter. Chill rounds in the freezer or freezing compartment of the refrigerator for about 5 minutes until firm. Place in between each section of tomato, arrange in center of serving dish and garnish with sprigs of parsley. Serve with Cheese Straws.

If preferred, the mixed vegetable salad may be bought ready prepared. The most suitable is Russian Salad.

Some cold meat choices to serve at a buffet.

Serve Ham Cornets with tasty cheese straws.

Hot appetizers

When the weather turns colder or when you tire of summer meals, a hot appetizer makes an interesting change. Many of the dishes in this section are classic appetizers, such as asparagus, soufflés and shellfish dishes. With the help of step-by-step pictures, we show you how surprisingly easy they are, even for the inexperienced cook.

Vegetables are often not considered by a hostess for a starter. However, fresh vegetables such as mushrooms, bell peppers, tomatoes and zucchini make delicious and refreshing dishes.

Pasta, served Italian style, is perfect to begin a meal. For example, serve small helpings of tagliatelle to begin a supper or dinner party. Pasta is also perfect when you are feeding large numbers, such as for a teenage party.

Mushrooms Baked in Cream.

Mushrooms Baked in Cream

3 cups mushrooms
1 egg
⅜ cup milk
2 thick slices of white bread
oil for deep fat frying
salt
few black peppercorns
3–4 tbsp finely chopped fresh parsley
⅜ cup light cream

Set the oven at 350°F.

Remove stalks from mushrooms and discard. Wipe mushrooms clean with a damp cloth, but do not peel. Set aside.

Beat the egg and milk together. Cut the bread into 4 inch rounds with a fluted cookie cutter and dip into the egg and milk mixture until coated. Deep fry in hot oil until golden brown, then drain on absorbent paper. Transfer to individual ovenproof plates or dishes. If you do not have ovenproof glass plates and cloches as shown, you can use ordinary heatproof plates and basins or bowls.

Pile the mushrooms on top of the fried bread and season with plenty of salt and finely crushed black peppercorns. Sprinkle with parsley. Pour the cream slowly over the mushrooms, then cover with an ovenproof glass cloche or bowl.

Bake in preset oven for 15–20 minutes, then serve immediately.

Mushroom Wheels

Wipe mushrooms clean with a damp cloth, but do not peel. Using the tip of a sharp pointed knife, cut curved grooves in the top of mushroom caps (trimmings can be used in casseroles, soups and stocks, etc.)

Brush mushroom caps with lemon juice to prevent discoloration, then fry gently for 1–2 minutes in equal quantities of hot oil and butter. Use as a garnish for chops, fish and steaks, etc.

Hot appetizers

An appetizing platter of Stuffed Zucchini and Tomatoes.

An appetizing platter of Stuffed Zucchini and Tomatoes.

Platter of Stuffed Zucchini and Tomatoes

For zucchini
4 small zucchini
1 clove of garlic
salt
¼ cup butter or margarine
¼ cup grated Gruyère or
  Emmenthaler cheese
2 heaped tbsp fresh white breadcrumbs
pepper
¼ cup grated Parmesan cheese

For tomatoes
3 medium tomatoes
2 heaped tbsp fresh brown breadcrumbs
1 tbsp chopped fresh herbs (parsley, chives,
  basil, marjoram etc.)
2 tbsp butter or margarine, softened
¼ tsp garlic salt
freshly ground black pepper to taste
a little basic garlic oil

Set the oven at 375°F.

Put the zucchini in the top of a steamer, cover and steam for about 10 minutes until tender but still firm. Cool, then cut in half lengthwise and scoop out flesh. Keep skins and flesh hot. Meanwhile, peel garlic and crush with a little salt. Soften half the butter or margarine and work into the garlic. Add garlic, grated cheese and breadcrumbs to the zucchini flesh. Stir well and add pepper to taste.

Spoon filling into zucchini skins and sprinkle with Parmesan. Dot with butter or margarine. Place on a cookie sheet.

Cut the tomatoes in half and scoop out the flesh. Discard pips and cores. Mix flesh with the remaining ingredients except garlic oil. Spoon filling into tomato cases and sprinkle with garlic oil. Place on a baking sheet.

Bake the zucchini and tomatoes in the preset oven for 12–15 minutes until browned. Serve hot.

Onions à la Bolognese

6 large mild onions
oil for sprinkling
6 sprigs rosemary (optional)

For sauce
1 medium onion
1 medium carrot
1 stalk of celery
1 tbsp oil
1 tbsp butter or margarine
¼ lb ground lean beef
¼ lb tomatoes
2 tsp tomato paste
¼ tsp sugar
¼ cup dry white wine
1¼ cups well flavored beef stock
1 tbsp finely chopped fresh parsley
salt and pepper

For filling
¼ lb cooked ground lean beef
1 tbsp tomato paste
1 tsp dried thyme
1 egg yolk
salt and pepper

Peel onions, place in a large pan of gently simmering salted water and simmer until just tender. Remove with a slotted spoon, leave until cool enough to handle, then cut out center flesh and reserve. Set onion cases aside.

To make the sauce, peel onion, chop carrot and celery finely. Heat oil and butter or margarine in a pan, add chopped vegetables and cook gently for about 5 minutes until lightly colored. Stir in the ground beef, mashing it down well with a wooden spoon. Cook gently until beef is browned, stirring occasionally.

Meanwhile, skin the tomatoes and chop the flesh roughly. Add to pan with remaining sauce ingredients and stir well to combine. Bring to the boil, then lower the heat and simmer, uncovered, for 25–30 minutes until thick.

Set oven at 350°F. To make the filling, put all ingredients in a bowl with reserved onion flesh. Stir to combine, mashing ingredients together with a wooden spoon. Fill into onion cases and place in a greased baking pan. Sprinkle onions with oil and bake in preset oven for 15–20 minutes.

Transfer baked onions to a warmed serving dish and pour in sauce. Garnish with sprigs of rosemary if liked. Serve hot.

Onions à la Bolognese make a delicious change.

Zucchini with Cheese

1 lb zucchini
2 tbsp oil
¼ cup butter or margarine
⅔ cup boiled long grain rice
½ cup grated Gruyère or Emmenthaler
  cheese
2 egg yolks
salt and pepper
⅔ cup fine fresh brown breadcrumbs
⅛ cup grated Parmesan cheese

Put the zucchini in the top of a steamer, cover with a lid and steam for about 10 minutes until tender. Remove from steamer, dice about threequarters and set aside. Slice the remainder finely into rounds.

Heat 1 tbsp oil and ¼ cup of butter or margarine in a frying pan. Add the diced zucchini and the rice and fry gently until golden, turning occasionally.

Add the grated Gruyère or Emmenthaler to the pan. Stir well until the cheese melts, then turn off the heat. Add the egg yolks and salt and pepper to taste and stir briskly with a wooden spoon to mix.

Transfer the mixture to a warmed heatproof serving dish. Mix the breadcrumbs with the grated Parmesan and sprinkle over the zucchini mixture. Dot with 2 tbsp butter or margarine and put under a preheated hot broiler until golden brown.

Meanwhile, heat the remaining butter or margarine and oil in the frying pan and fry the reserved sliced zucchini until golden. Remove from pan with a slotted spoon and use to garnish the edge of the serving dish. Serve immediately.

Garlic Oil

Basic Recipe

1 lb garlic cloves
5 cups olive or corn oil

Peel and crush the cloves of garlic. Put in a jar (stone or earthenware if possible) and pour over the oil. Cover with a lid or several layers of foil. Leave for about 1 week, stirring every day, then leave in a cool place for about 1 month without disturbing. Strain into screwtopped jars and keep as for ordinary oil. Use as a salad oil, in dressings and mayonnaise.

Anchovy Butter

Basic Recipe

1 × 2 oz can of anchovies in oil
milk
½ cup butter
1–2 tsp lemon juice
freshly ground black pepper
few drops of pink food coloring (optional)

Drain the anchovies and put in a bowl. Cover with milk and leave to soak for at least 30 minutes.

Meanwhile, beat the butter until soft and light. Drain the anchovies and pat dry with absorbent paper. Put in a mortar or bowl and pound to a paste with a pestle or kitchen mallet.

Beat anchovy paste into butter with lemon juice and black pepper to taste. Stir in food coloring to make mixture a very pale pink, if liked.

Use while still soft as a stuffing, or for piping around the edge of finished dishes. To make into pats, flatten between 2 sheets of waxed paper. Chill in the refrigerator until firm, then stamp into small shapes using a cookie cutter.

This is a delicious stuffing for fish, peppers, tomatoes etc., or piped around the edge of finished dishes to make an attractive garnish. Serve anchovy butter pats ice cold on hot fish dishes.

Serve Zucchini with Cheese as an appetizer or a vegetable dish.

Ratatouille with Scrambled Eggs.

Ratatouille with Scrambled Eggs

For ratatouille
2 medium eggplants
salt
1 large mild onion
1 clove of garlic
2 large sweet peppers
4 small zucchini
½ lb ripe tomatoes
3 tbsp olive oil
pepper
2 tbsp finely chopped fresh parsley

For scrambled eggs
4 eggs
6 tbsp milk
¼ cup butter or margarine

Slice the eggplant finely, sprinkle with salt and leave for 30 minutes to extract the juices.

Peel the onion and chop finely. Peel the garlic and crush with ½ tsp salt. Cut the tops off the peppers and scoop out the pith and seeds. Chop the flesh finely. Slice the zucchini finely into rounds. Skin the tomatoes and chop roughly.

Heat the oil in a saucepan, add the onion, garlic and chopped peppers and fry gently for about 5 minutes until lightly colored. Add the zucchini and fry for a further 5 minutes, stirring occasionally.

Meanwhile, wash the eggplant slices under cold running water, then pat dry with absorbent paper. Add to the pan and cook for 5 minutes, stirring occasionally. Stir in the tomatoes and bring the mixture to the boil. Lower the heat, cover tightly and simmer gently for about 30 minutes until the vegetables are soft and juicy, stirring occasionally. Add salt and pepper to taste and stir in the chopped parsley. Transfer to a warmed serving dish or individual bowls and keep hot.

Beat the eggs and milk together and season to taste with salt and pepper. Melt the butter or margarine in a pan, pour in the eggs and milk and scramble over low heat, stirring constantly. Spoon on top of ratatouille and serve immediately.

HOW TO COOK ASPARAGUS

1. Trim asparagus spears to equal lengths by cutting off hard ends. Scrape from below the tips to the end of the stems. Wash under cold running water.

2. Stand the asparagus spears upright in the inner perforated container of an asparagus cooker.

3. Stand the inner container inside the outer pan. Pour in gently bubbling salted water, keeping tips above the level of the water. Cover and simmer gently for 10–15 minutes until tender. Remove inner container, transfer asparagus to a warmed serving platter and serve hot with melted butter or Hollandaise sauce. If you do not have an asparagus cooker, then use a tall narrow saucepan filled with gently bubbling salted water.

Hot appetizers

Moroccan Peppers

If liked, canned pimientos and tomatoes can be used instead of fresh.

2 large red bell peppers
1 large mild onion
1 lb ripe tomatoes
¼ cup butter or margarine
1 tsp finely chopped fresh basil,
  or ½ tsp dried basil
salt and pepper
3 eggs
4 tbsp fresh light cream or top of the milk

Cut the pimientos in halves and remove the pith, seeds and skin. Slice the flesh thinly. Peel the onion and slice into thin rings. Skin the tomatoes, then slice finely.

Melt half the butter or margarine in a pan, add the prepared vegetables and cover with a lid. Cook very gently for about 20 minutes until the vegetables are soft and juicy. Stir in the basil with salt and pepper to taste. Transfer to a warmed serving dish and keep hot.

Beat the eggs and cream or milk together and season to taste with salt and pepper. Melt the remaining butter or margarine in a pan, pour in the egg mixture and scramble over low heat, stirring constantly. Spoon in a line down the center of hot vegetables and serve immediately with hot French bread or fingers of hot buttered toast.

Mushroom and Onion Flan

basic savory shortcrust pastry
  made from 1 cup of flour
½ lb shallots or small onions
5 tbsp butter or margarine
3 tbsp oil
3 cups mushrooms
2 eggs
1¼ cups heavy cream
¼ cup flour
dash of paprika
salt and pepper

Set the oven at 350°F.

Roll out pastry and line a 7–8 inch diameter flan ring placed on a greased cookie sheet. Chill. Peel and chop shallots or onions.

Melt 3 tbsp butter and the oil in a skillet, add the chopped shallots or onions and sauté until transparent, but not browned. Remove onions with a slotted spoon, place in a sieve and press over the skillet so the juices drip through. Add the rest of the butter, wipe and slice mushrooms very thinly, then add to pan. Sauté lightly until cooked and season with salt and pepper. Add to shallots and spread over base of flan case.

Beat the eggs in a bowl, add the cream and mix well. In a smaller bowl, add the flour to about 2–3 tbsp of the egg and cream mixture and stir until smooth. Return this to the rest of the egg and cream mixture and stir to mix. Add paprika, adjust seasoning and pour over mushrooms and onions in the flan case. Bake in the preset oven for 45–50 minutes. Chill.

Tomatoes Bonne Femme

8 large firm tomatoes
1 small onion
1 clove of garlic
4 slices of bacon
1½ cups mushrooms
3 tbsp butter or margarine
1 tbsp vegetable oil
⅓–⅔ cup fine fresh white breadcrumbs
½ tsp dried basil
salt and pepper
⅛ cup grated Parmesan cheese

To serve
1¼ cups basic tomato sauce
triangles of fried bread croûtons (optional)

Set the oven at 400°F.

Cut the tops off the tomatoes, hollow out the insides and reserve flesh. Set tomato cases aside on a cookie sheet.

Peel the onion and chop finely. Crush the garlic. Cut the rind from the bacon and discard. Dice bacon finely. Wipe the mushrooms clean with a damp cloth, but do not peel. Chop finely.

Heat 2 tbsp butter or margarine and the oil in a pan. Add the onion, garlic and bacon and fry for about 5 minutes until golden. Stir in the mushrooms and reserved tomato flesh. Cook for a further 2 minutes, then transfer to a bowl. Stir in the breadcrumbs, basil and salt and pepper to taste and mix all ingredients thoroughly.

Spoon prepared filling into tomato cases. Sprinkle with grated Parmesan cheese and dot with remaining butter or margarine. Bake in the preset oven for 8–10 minutes or until hot. Meanwhile, heat tomato sauce gently.

Transfer tomatoes to a warmed serving platter and garnish with croûtons, if liked. Serve the tomato sauce separately.

Tomatoes Bonne Femme.

Mushroom and Cheese Vol-au-Vents.

Mushroom and Cheese Vol-au-Vents

For these vol-au-vents you will need to make up half a batch of basic puff pastry or you can buy readymade fresh or frozen vol-au-vent cases.

8 cooked and cooled vol-au-vent cases
2 cups mushrooms
¼ cup dry white wine or
   chicken stock
salt and pepper
3 hardcooked eggs
2½ cups basic Mornay sauce

To garnish
few sprigs of watercress

Set the oven at 325°F.

Remove lids from vol-au-vents to expose cavity and set aside on a cookie sheet.

Wipe the mushrooms clean with a damp cloth, but do not peel. Chop very finely. Put in a pan with the wine or stock and salt and pepper to taste. Simmer gently for 5 minutes.

Meanwhile, sieve the hardcooked eggs. Remove mushrooms from heat and fold into the Mornay sauce with the sieved eggs. Mix well and taste for seasoning.

Fill vol-au-vents with sauce and cover loosely with foil. Bake in the preset oven for 15–20 minutes or until vol-au-vents and filling are hot. Meanwhile, heat remaining sauce gently.

Transfer vol-au-vents to a warmed serving platter and garnish with sprigs of watercress. Serve hot sauce separately.

Tomato Sauce

1 small onion
1 clove of garlic
salt
2 tbsp olive or corn oil
1 lb ripe tomatoes
¼ tsp dried oregano
¼ tsp dried basil
1 tbsp wine vinegar
3 tbsp stock or water
pinch of sugar
freshly ground black pepper

Peel the onion and chop finely. Peel the garlic and crush with ½ tsp salt. Heat the oil in a saucepan, add the onion and garlic and cook gently for about 5 minutes until lightly colored.

Meanwhile, chop the tomatoes roughly. Add to the pan with the remaining ingredients. Simmer gently until the tomatoes are soft and juicy, stirring occasionally.

Remove from the heat and strain. Return to rinsed out pan and reheat gently. Taste for seasoning and serve hot.

Use for coating fish, meat, poultry or vegetables, or as a base for many Italian dishes.

Skinning Tomatoes

If you have a gas stove, this method is quick and easy. Push a fork firmly into the tomato. Hold over flame on top of stove until skin scorches and splits. Leave to cool slightly, then peel off the skin with your fingers.

If you have an electric stove or if you are skinning a large quantity, plunge the tomatoes into boiling water for a few seconds, then into ice cold water. Peel as for the first method.

Peeling Peppers

Cut the pepper in half lengthwise. Remove all pith and seeds. Place under a preheated hot broiler, skin side uppermost.

Remove from the broiler when the skin begins to split and become charred. Hold pepper halves in a cloth and peel away the skin with a sharp knife.

Hot appetizers

Mushroom Fritters with Tartare Sauce is an unusual appetizer.

Mushroom Fritters with Tartare Sauce

For tartare sauce
2 hardcooked eggs
1¼ cups basic mayonnaise
1 tbsp chopped capers
1 tbsp chopped gherkins
1 tbsp chopped chives
2 tsp lemon juice
salt and pepper

For mushroom fritters
3 cups fresh button mushrooms or
    1 × 7 oz can button mushrooms
oil for deep fat frying
1½ cups flour
½ tsp salt
2 tbsp vegetable oil
about 1 cup cold water
2 egg whites

Fritters must be served immediately after cooking, therefore the tartare sauce should be made first. To make tartare sauce: sieve the hardcooked eggs and stir into the mayonnaise with the remaining sauce ingredients. Taste for seasoning and stir until evenly mixed. Spoon into a serving bowl or jug, cover and keep in a cool place while making fritters.

Wipe the fresh mushrooms clean with a damp cloth, but do not peel. Remove stalks and discard. If using canned mushrooms, drain well. Set aside.

Sift the flour and salt into a bowl. Make a well in the center and pour in the oil and half the water. Stir the flour gradually into the oil and water until a smooth batter is formed. Beat in more water until the batter forms a coating consistency. Beat the egg whites until stiff and fold into the batter with a metal spoon. Dip the mushrooms one by one into the batter, making sure that they are evenly coated.

Heat the oil in a deep fat fryer until it is hot enough to turn a stale bread cube golden in 20–30 seconds.

Put a few mushrooms at a time into the hot oil and deep fry until golden, turning them during cooking. Remove from pan with a slotted spoon and drain on absorbent paper. Keep hot in the oven on a warmed serving platter while frying remainder. Serve immediately with tartare sauce.

Greek Spinach and Cheese Puffs

8 oz package of frozen chopped spinach
basic puff pastry made from 2 cups flour
2 tbsp softened butter or margarine
⅔ of an 8 oz package cream cheese
¼ tsp ground nutmeg
salt and pepper
1 egg
1 egg white
oil for deep fat frying

To serve
plain unsweetened yogurt or
    cultured sour cream

Put the frozen spinach in a colander or sieve and leave to thaw and drain. Meanwhile, roll out the pastry as thinly as possible on a floured board and cut into about 24 4 inch squares. Set aside.

Put the spinach in a bowl with the butter or margarine, cream cheese, nutmeg and salt and pepper to taste. Beat well until thoroughly combined, then beat in the egg to bind.

Divide the mixture equally between the squares of pastry putting spoonfuls in *one* corner of each square so that the pastry can fold over the filling to form a triangular shape.

Brush the edges of the pastry with the egg white, then fold over into triangles, pressing the edges down well and pinching them to seal.

Heat the oil in a deep fat fryer until it is hot enough to turn a stale bread cube golden in 20–30 seconds. Put in a few triangles at a time and fry until golden brown on both sides, turning once. Drain on absorbent paper and keep hot.

Serve yogurt or sour cream separately.

Greek Spinach and Cheese Puffs.

Cheese Soufflés with a difference!

Cheese Soufflés in Pastry

¼ cup butter or margarine
basic puff pastry made from 1½ cups flour
1 egg
¼ cup + 1 tbsp flour
1¼ cups hot milk
¾ cup grated Parmesan cheese
dash of ground nutmeg
salt and pepper
5 egg whites

Set the oven at 425°F.

Soften a quarter of the butter or margarine and use to brush the insides of 4 individual dishes about 4½ inches in diameter.

Roll out the pastry on a floured board and cut into 4 squares large enough to fit inside the dishes. Put the squares in the dishes, pressing them down in the middle so that the 4 corners protrude above the rim of each dish. Beat the whole egg and use to brush the pastry. Stand the dishes on a cookie sheet and set aside.

Melt the remaining butter or margarine in a large pan. Stir in the flour with a wooden spoon and cook gently for 1–2 minutes until the mixture forms a soft ball, stirring constantly.

Remove pan from heat and gradually stir in the hot milk, beating vigorously all the time to obtain a smooth sauce. When all the milk is incorporated, return pan to heat and bring to the boil, stirring constantly.

Lower the heat and add the seasonings. Simmer gently until the sauce thickens, stirring constantly. Remove pan from heat and stir in the cheese.

Beat the egg whites until stiff. Fold into the sauce until evenly distributed. Divide soufflé mixture between prepared dishes. Bake in preset oven on shelf above center for 10–15 minutes until well risen and golden brown. Serve immediately.

Cheese Soufflés in Pastry are delicious both as an appetizer and as a supper dish. For supper, serve them with a green salad on the side and French bread.

Individual Soufflé Tomatoes.

Soufflé Tomatoes

12 large tomatoes
3 tbsp butter or margarine
¼ cup + 1 tbsp flour
1¼ cups hot milk
¾ cup mature Cheddar-type cheese
1 tsp anchovy flavoring
pepper
5 egg whites

To garnish
1–2 tbsp chopped chives

Set the oven at 400°F.

Cut the tops off the tomatoes, scoop out all flesh, seeds and central cores and discard (or use in casseroles, soups, stock, etc.). Put the tomato cases on a cookie sheet and set aside.

Melt the butter or margarine in a large pan. Stir in the flour with a wooden spoon and cook gently for 1–2 minutes until the mixture forms a soft ball, stirring constantly.

Remove pan from heat and gradually stir in the hot milk, beating vigorously all the time to obtain a smooth sauce. When all the milk is incorporated, return pan to heat and bring to the boil, stirring constantly.

Lower the heat and simmer gently. Grate the cheese and add to the pan with the anchovy flavoring and pepper to taste. Stir constantly until the cheese melts and the sauce is thick and smooth. Remove pan from heat.

Beat the egg whites until stiff. Fold into the sauce until evenly distributed. Spoon into prepared tomato cases. Bake in the preset oven on shelf above center for 15 minutes until well risen and golden brown. Transfer to a warmed serving dish, sprinkle with chopped chives and serve immediately.

Allow 2 tomatoes per person if you are serving them as an appetizer. Serve thin slices of buttered brown bread on the side. They are also delicious as a vegetable dish, especially with fish, broiled meats and chicken. Allow 2–3 per person.

Cheese Soufflé with Eggs

¼ cup butter or margarine
¼ cup + 1 tbsp flour
1¼ cups hot milk
¾ cup grated Gruyère or Emmenthaler
   cheese
¼ tsp powdered English mustard
salt and pepper
5 egg whites
4 eggs
¼ cup grated Parmesan cheese

Soften a quarter of the butter or margarine and use to brush the inside of a 4
cup soufflé dish. Set aside.

Melt the remaining butter or margarine
in a large pan. Stir in the flour with a
wooden spoon and cook gently for 1–2
minutes until the mixture forms a soft ball,
stirring constantly.

Remove pan from heat and gradually
stir in the hot milk, beating vigorously all
the time to obtain a smooth sauce. When
all the milk is incorporated, return pan to
heat and bring to the boil, stirring constantly.

Lower the heat and simmer gently. Add
the grated Gruyère or Emmenthaler to
the pan with the mustard and salt and
pepper to taste. Stir constantly until the
cheese melts and the sauce is thick and
smooth. Remove pan from heat.

Beat the egg whites until stiff. Fold into
the sauce until evenly distributed. Spoon
half the mixture into the prepared soufflé
dish. Make 4 indentations in the mixture
and break in the eggs one by one. Cover

with the remaining soufflé mixture and
sprinkle with Parmesan cheese.

Bake in preset oven on center shelf for
30–35 minutes until well risen and golden
brown. Serve immediately with grated
Parmesan cheese.

Croque Monsieur

For each portion
2 slices white bread
1 tbsp butter
2 slices Gruyère or Emmenthaler cheese
   to fit bread slice
1 slice cooked ham to fit bread slice

Trim crusts from bread slices and lightly
spread with butter. Lay a slice of cheese on
one slice of the buttered bread. Place the
slice of ham on top, add the second slice of
cheese and top with the second slice of
buttered bread. Broil on both sides until
toasted and golden brown, and the cheese
has melted. Serve hot.

Eggs Florentine.

Eggs Florentine

8 oz package frozen chopped spinach
¼ cup softened butter or margarine
good dash ground nutmeg
salt and pepper
6 eggs
6 tbsp light cream or creamy milk
¼ cup grated Cheddar cheese

Set the oven at 350°F.

Put the frozen spinach in a colander or
sieve and leave to thaw and drain.

Brush the insides of 6 3 inch diameter
soufflé dishes with a quarter of the butter
or margarine. Mix the spinach with the
nutmeg and salt and pepper. Beat in the
remaining butter or margarine until evenly distributed.

Divide spinach equally between the
buttered dishes and hollow out the centers
slightly. Break 1 egg into each hollow and
pour 1 tbsp cream or milk over each.
Sprinkle the cheese over the top with a
little salt and pepper.

Cheese Soufflé with Eggs.

Stand the dishes in a roasting pan half filled with hot water and cover with buttered foil. Bake in preset oven for 20–25 minutes until eggs are set.

Scrambled Eggs with Shrimps

2 slices white bread, ½ inch thick
a little oil or butter for frying
2 tbsp butter
3 eggs
2–3 tbsp milk
salt and white pepper
¼ cup peeled shrimps

For decoration, you can cut the bread slices with an oval cutter. Fry bread slices in oil or butter until golden brown. Drain on absorbent paper and keep hot.

Melt the butter in a pan over low heat, break eggs into a bowl, add milk and whisk briskly. Season with salt and white pepper and pour eggs into pan, stirring with a wooden spoon. As soon as they are lightly set, take pan off heat and stir in the shrimps. Adjust seasoning and heap on to fried bread base.

The base and 'top' for the scrambled eggs are cut with an oval cookie cutter. Half the shrimps were folded into the eggs and the rest were placed round the bread croûte to decorate.

Smoked eel makes a luxury variation of this simple dish. A few chopped chives add a colorful and tasty garnish, too.

Cheese Croquettes

¾ lb potatoes, boiled
2 tbsp butter or margarine
1½ cups grated Cheddar cheese
2 egg yolks, beaten
¼ cup flour
⅜ cup fresh white breadcrumbs
1 egg, beaten
salt and pepper

Mash potatoes well. When cool, beat in butter or margarine and chill. Then beat cheese and egg yolks into the potato and season. Chill again until firm.

Roll out the mixture into a long thin strip about 1½ inches in diameter. Dip each croquette first into flour, then beaten egg and then breadcrumbs. Chill again for about 30 minutes.

Heat oil in a deep fat frier and fry until golden brown.

Eggs Baked in Pastry

3 tbsp butter or margarine
basic puff pastry made from 1 cup of flour
7 eggs
6 bacon slices
1 tsp black peppercorns
salt
6 tbsp light cream
2 tbsp finely chopped fresh parsley

Set the oven at 350°F.

Soften ⅓ of the butter or margarine and use to brush the insides of 6 individual soufflé or ramekin dishes.

Roll out the pastry on a floured board and cut into 6 squares large enough to fit inside the dishes. Put the squares in the dishes, pressing them down in the middle so that the 4 corners protrude above the rim of each dish. Beat 1 egg and use to brush the pastry. Stand the dishes on a cookie sheet and set aside.

Cut the rind off the bacon and discard. Dice bacon finely. Melt remaining butter or margarine in a pan, put in the bacon and fry for about 5 minutes until crisp and golden. Remove from pan with a slotted spoon and divide equally amongst the dishes. Sprinkle the bacon with pepper, then break 1 egg into each dish and sprinkle with salt. Pour 1 tbsp cream over each egg and sprinkle with parsley.

Bake in the preset oven for about 20–25 minutes until eggs are set, then remove from oven and serve immediately.

As a variation, these baked eggs may be taken out of their cooking dishes and served chilled. Allow them to become cold after baking, then chill in the refrigerator until quite firm before transferring pastry cases to a serving platter.

Eggs Baked in Pastry can be eaten hot or cold.

Cannelloni with Veal and Mushroom Stuffing

14 cannelloni tubes or pasta squares
2 tbsp oil
1 small onion
1 clove of garlic
salt
¼ lb finely ground lean veal
1¼ cups mushrooms
2 tbsp tomato paste
¼ tsp sugar
½ tsp dried oregano
pepper
a little stock or water
1 small egg
2 tbsp butter or margarine, softened
prepared Spinach and Cheese Sauce

To serve
grated Parmesan cheese

Put the cannelloni or pasta squares into a large pan of boiling salted water with 1 tsp oil. Cook for 8–10 minutes until tender. Lift out with a slotted spoon and leave to drain.

Peel the onion and chop finely. Peel the garlic and crush with ½ tsp salt. Heat the remaining oil in a pan, add the onion and garlic and fry gently for about 5 minutes until lightly colored.

Add the veal and fry gently for a further 10 minutes until browned, turning and stirring constantly.

Meanwhile, wipe the mushrooms clean with a damp cloth, but do not peel. Chop finely. Stir into the pan with the tomato paste, sugar, oregano and pepper to taste. Stir well to combine. Moisten with a little stock or water, cover with a lid and simmer gently for about 10 minutes, stirring occasionally. Remove from heat, taste for seasoning and stir in the egg.

Set the oven at 350°F. Spoon prepared filling into cannelloni tubes or divide equally amongst squares of pasta and roll up. Brush the inside of a shallow ovenproof dish with butter or margarine. Place the cannelloni in the dish in 2 layers.

Spoon over the prepared Spinach and Cheese Sauce and bake in the preset oven for about 15–20 minutes until the sauce is bubbling. Serve with grated Parmesan cheese.

Stuffed Cannelloni with Spinach and Cheese Sauce.

Spinach and Cheese Sauce

¼ lb package of frozen chopped spinach
¼ cup grated Parmesan cheese
2¼ cups hot basic white sauce
salt and pepper
1 tbsp butter or margarine

Put the frozen spinach in a colander or sieve and leave to thaw and drain.

Stir the spinach and cheese into the hot white sauce over a gentle heat. Simmer until the cheese melts, stirring constantly.

Add salt and pepper to taste, then beat in the butter or margarine. Use immediately.

This sauce is delicious with pasta dishes, such as Cannelloni with Veal and Mushroom Stuffing.

Ribbon pasta with Mushroom Topping.

Tagliatelle covered with Simple Tomato Sauce.

Mushroom Topping for Pasta

1 medium onion
1 clove of garlic
salt
¼ cup butter or margarine
1 tbsp olive oil
6 bacon slices
3 cups button mushrooms
2 tsp flour
4 tbsp well flavored stock
¼ tsp dried oregano
pepper

To finish
2 tbsp butter or margarine
1 cup button mushrooms
2 tbsp heavy cream
1–2 tbsp finely chopped fresh parsley
grated Parmesan cheese

Peel the onion and chop very finely. Peel the garlic and crush with ½ tsp salt. Heat the butter or margarine and oil in a pan, add the onion and garlic and fry gently for about 5 minutes until lightly colored.

Meanwhile, cut the rind off the bacon and discard. Dice bacon finely, then add to the pan and fry until browned.

Wipe the mushrooms clean with a damp cloth, but do not peel. Slice finely, then add to the pan. Fry until the juices run, and they are lightly colored.

Sprinkle the flour over the mushroom mixture and cook for 1–2 minutes, stirring constantly. Stir in the stock, add oregano and pepper to taste. Simmer gently.

To finish, melt the 2 tbsp butter or margarine in a separate pan. Add cleaned whole mushrooms and fry until lightly colored. Stir in the cream and parsley.

Serve hot mushroom sauce on a bed of freshly cooked pasta and top with mushrooms, cream and parsley. Serve with grated Parmesan cheese.

Tagliatelle with Simple Tomato Sauce

For sauce
2 lb ripe tomatoes
1 medium onion
1 clove of garlic
salt
4 tbsp olive oil
2 tsp finely chopped fresh oregano
  or 1 tsp dried oregano
dash of sugar
pepper

To serve
½ lb green tagliatelle
1 tsp vegetable oil
grated Parmesan cheese

Skin the tomatoes and chop the flesh roughly. Peel the onion and chop finely. Peel the garlic and crush with ½ tsp salt.

Heat the oil in a pan, add the onion and garlic and fry gently for about 5 minutes until lightly colored.

Add the chopped tomatoes to the pan with the oregano, sugar and pepper to taste. Simmer gently for about 20 minutes until the sauce is thick and reduced, stirring occasionally.

Meanwhile, put the tagliatelle in a large pan of boiling salted water with the vegetable oil. Cook for 8–10 minutes until tender, then drain and arrange in a warmed serving dish. Taste sauce for seasoning. If a smooth sauce is preferred, then purée sauce in an electric blender, or work through a foodmill or sieve. Reheat. Pour over the tagliatelle. Serve hot with grated Parmesan cheese.

Hot appetizers

Bolognese Sauce for Pasta

¼ lb sliced bacon
1 medium onion
1 medium carrot
2 stalks celery
2 cloves of garlic
2 tbsp butter or margarine
2 tbsp olive oil
½ lb ground lean beef
¼ lb chicken livers
1 tbsp tomato paste
dash of sugar
1¼ cups well flavored beef stock and
    ¾ cup dry white wine, or 2 cups stock
½ tsp dried oregano

½ tsp dried basil
salt and pepper

To serve
grated Parmesan cheese

Cut the rind off the bacon and discard. Dice bacon finely. Peel the onion and carrot and chop finely with the celery. Crush the garlic.

Heat the butter or margarine and oil in a pan, add the bacon and fry until crisp and golden. Remove from pan with a slotted spoon and set aside.

Add vegetables and garlic to the pan and fry gently for about 5 minutes until lightly colored. Add the beef and fry for a further 10 minutes until browned, turning and stirring occasionally.

Meanwhile, chop the chicken livers and stir into the beef. Return the bacon to the pan and stir in the tomato paste and sugar. Add remaining ingredients and stir well to mix.

Simmer sauce for 25–30 minutes until thick and reduced, stirring occasionally. Taste for seasoning. Serve hot on a bed of freshly cooked spaghetti or pasta bows, with grated Parmesan cheese. For a richer sauce, stir in ⅓ cup cream just before serving.

Veal and Mushroom Sauce for Pasta

1 medium onion
1 medium carrot
2 stalks celery
1 cup mushrooms
2 tbsp butter or margarine
2 tbsp olive oil
½ lb ground lean veal
2 large tomatoes
1 tbsp flour
1 cup well flavored chicken stock
⅔ cup dry white wine
1 tsp finely chopped fresh oregano
    or ½ tsp dried oregano
salt and pepper

To serve
grated Parmesan cheese

Peel the onion and chop finely. Peel the carrot and dice finely with the celery. Wipe the mushrooms clean with a damp cloth, but do not peel. Chop finely.

Heat the butter or margarine and oil in a pan, add the vegetables and fry gently for about 5 minutes until lightly colored. Add the veal and fry for a further 10 minutes until browned, turning and stirring constantly.

Meanwhile, skin the tomatoes and chop the flesh roughly. Stir into the veal until evenly mixed. Sprinkle the flour into the pan and cook for 1–2 minutes, stirring constantly. Stir in the stock gradually with a wooden spoon, then add the wine, oregano and salt and pepper to taste.

Simmer sauce for 25–30 minutes until thick and reduced, stirring occasionally. Taste for seasoning. Serve hot on a bed of freshly cooked pasta shells, with grated Parmesan cheese.

A tasty Bolognese Sauce for pasta.

Pasta shells with Veal and Mushroom Sauce.

HOW TO MAKE AND STORE PANCAKES

Basic Pancake Batter

1 cup flour
pinch of salt
1 egg
1¼ cups milk
vegetable oil for frying

Sift the flour and salt into a bowl and make a well in the center. Beat the egg and put into the well. Add half the milk gradually, beating all the time with a wooden spoon to draw in the flour from the sides.

Pour in the remaining milk and 1–2 drops of oil and beat vigorously to make a smooth, creamy batter. Transfer batter to a jug.

Pancakes Mornay

4 basic pancakes
½ cup chopped shrimps
⅔ small package of cream cheese
¼ cup light cream
salt and pepper
1¼ cups basic Mornay sauce
1 tbsp butter or margarine
about ¼ cup grated Parmesan
¼ cup whole shrimps

Mix chopped shrimps and cream cheese with a little cream. Season. Spread 1–2 tbsp over half

1. Brush both sides of a large piece of waxed paper with oil.

2. Brush the inside of pancake pan with a little oil, put over a low heat until pan becomes very hot.

of each pancake. Fold.

Grease an ovenproof dish and put in the pancakes. Mix remaining cream into Mornay sauce and pour over the pancakes. Sprinkle with Parmesan. Decorate with whole shrimps. Bake for 15–20 minutes.

Pancakes Mornay decorated with whole shrimps.

3. Stir pancake batter to mix. Lift pan off heat and pour in a little batter at the side of the pan.

4. Tip the pan quickly from side to side so that the batter runs over the entire base. Return to heat and cook until mixture sets and the underneath becomes golden.

5. Turn the pancake over carefully, using a palette knife.

6. Slide pancake out onto oiled waxed paper. Continue making pancakes in this way until all the batter is used.

7. Cut waxed paper into squares to put between pancakes, then pile one on top of the other. Wrap the pancakes in foil and store in refrigerator or freezer until required.

Shellfish Pancakes

Although this recipe uses mussels, prawns and crab, any other kind of seafood may be substituted with equally good results.

6 basic pancakes
¼ cup cooked shelled mussels
¼ cup shelled and veined prawns
¾ cup frozen crabmeat, thawed
¼ cup butter or margarine
¼ cup + 1 tbsp flour
¾ cup hot basic fish stock
   and ½ cup dry white wine
   or 1¼ cups hot fish stock
⅔ cup heavy cream
2 tsp tomato paste
salt and pepper
2 tbsp finely chopped parsley

Set the oven at 375°F.

Lay the pancakes flat on a board or table. Chop the mussels and prawns roughly. Flake the crabmeat. Set aside.

Melt threequarters of the butter or margarine in a pan. Stir in the flour with a wooden spoon and cook gently for 1–2 minutes until the mixture forms a soft ball, stirring constantly.

Remove pan from heat and gradually stir in ¾ cup hot stock, beating vigorously all the time to obtain a smooth sauce. Beat in the white wine or remaining fish stock. Return pan to the heat and bring to the boil, stirring constantly.

Lower the heat, stir in the cream, tomato paste and salt and pepper to taste. Bring to the boil again, then lower the heat and simmer until the sauce thickens, stirring constantly. Remove from the heat and fold in the prepared shellfish with half the parsley.

Put 1–2 tbsp of sauce at one end of each pancake and roll up to enclose. Brush the inside of a shallow ovenproof dish or individual dishes with the remaining butter or margarine. Place pancakes in dish(es) and pour over remaining sauce.

Bake in the preset oven for 10–15 minutes until pancakes are hot and sauce is bubbling. Sprinkle with remaining parsley and serve immediately straight from the baking dish(es).

Shrimp Pancakes for a special occasion.

Shrimp Pancakes

6 basic pancakes
¼ lb shelled and veined shrimps
⅔ cup heavy cream
finely grated rind of 1 lemon
1 tsp finely crushed black peppercorns
2 hardcooked eggs
1 tbsp finely chopped parsley
salt
1 tbsp butter or margarine

Set the oven at 375°F.

Lay the pancakes flat on a board or table. Chop the shrimps roughly, reserving a few whole ones for the garnish.

Put the cream in a pan with the lemon rind and crushed peppercorns and bring slowly to the boil. Remove from the heat. Chop the eggs finely and stir into the cream with the parsley and a little salt.

Put 1–2 tbsp of chopped shrimps at one end of each pancake, moisten with a little of the cream mixture and roll up to enclose the shrimps completely.

Brush the base of a shallow ovenproof dish with butter or margarine and put in the pancakes. Pour over the remaining cream mixture and garnish with reserved whole shrimps. Bake in preset oven for 10–12 minutes until hot, then brown under a preheated hot broiler for a few minutes. Serve hot straight from the baking dish.

For a special occasion this starter can be served with extra shrimps broiled on skewers. Allow 1 skewer per person.

Mussel Pancakes.

Mussel Pancakes

4 basic pancakes
24 fresh mussels
¼ cup dry white wine or cider
¼ cup water
1 strip of lemon peel
4 black peppercorns
2 sprigs parsley
⅔ cup heavy cream
1 tbsp butter or margarine

Scrub mussels thoroughly under cold running water. Discard beards and any mussels that are open. Soak cleaned mussels for 1 hour in cold water, then drain.

Put mussels in a pan with the wine or cider, water, lemon peel, peppercorns and parsley stalks. Bring to the boil, then lower the heat and cover with a lid. Simmer for 5–7 minutes until the mussels open.

Remove from pan and discard any that are still closed. Set aside. Boil cooking liquid in pan until reduced to a scant ½ cup.

Set the oven at 350°F. Stir the cream into the reduced cooking liquid and simmer until heated through. Brush an oven-proof serving platter with the butter or margarine. Place 1 pancake on the dish and fold in half. Put a quarter of the mussels in center of the pancake, spoon over a little sauce, then fold over the sides of pancake to form a parcel. Repeat with remaining pancakes and mussels.

Cover the platter with foil. Bake in the preset oven for 7–10 minutes until heated through. Chop the parsley finely and use to garnish pancakes. Serve immediately with any remaining hot cream sauce.

Blini, a classic Russian dish.

Blini

1 package active dry yeast
6 tbsp lukewarm water
scant 1¼ cups milk
2¼ cups buckwheat flour
2 eggs
2 tbsp melted butter or margarine
1 tsp sugar
½ tsp salt
butter or vegetable oil for frying

Sprinkle the yeast over the lukewarm water. Leave in a warm place for 15–20 minutes until frothy. Meanwhile, heat about half of the milk to blood heat.

Sift half the flour into a warmed bowl, make a well in the center and pour in the frothy yeast liquid and the warmed milk. Beat vigorously with a wooden spoon until a smooth batter is formed, gradually drawing in the flour from the sides.

Cover the bowl and leave in a warm place for about 2 hours until almost doubled in bulk.

Heat the remaining milk to blood heat. Beat into the batter with the remaining flour a little at a time. Separate the eggs and beat in the yolks with the melted butter or margarine, sugar and salt. Leave to rise again for 30 minutes–1 hour until almost doubled in bulk.

Beat the egg whites until stiff, then fold into the batter with a large metal spoon. Leave to rise again for about 30 minutes.

Heat a little butter or oil in a small skillet and, when hot, pour in 2 tbsp batter to make a pancake about 4 inches in diameter. Fry for 1–2 minutes until golden on underside, then turn over and fry on the other side. Transfer to a warm oven and keep hot while frying remainder. Heat more butter or oil before adding fresh batter to the pan.

When all the blini are cooked, pile them up on a warmed serving platter.

These Russian pancakes are traditionally served with caviare, but are equally good eaten with pickled herrings, sour cream, yogurt and lemon wedges.

Hot appetizers

Clams Mornay

If fresh clams are unobtainable, this recipe can be made equally well with fresh mussels.

12 fresh soft clams
salt
1¼ cups dry white wine or basic fish stock
about 1¼ cups creamy milk
6 tbsp butter or margarine
¼ cup flour
¼ cup grated Gruyère or Emmenthaler cheese
pepper
2–3 tbsp fine dry breadcrumbs
¼ cup grated Parmesan cheese
1 tbsp chopped chives
2 tsp finely chopped parsley

Scrub clams thoroughly under cold running water. Discard any that are open or which do not close when tapped sharply. Soak for 1 hour in lightly salted cold water, then drain.

Put clams in a pan with the wine or stock. Bring to the boil, then lower the heat and cover with a lid. Simmer for 6–8 minutes or until clams open.

Remove from pan and discard any that are still closed. Strain cooking liquid into a measuring jug. Remove meat from clam shells, discarding any black outer webbing if present. Reserve shells. Chop the meat very finely and set aside with the shells. Pour clam liquor into the measuring jug and make up to 1¼ cups with milk; leave to one side.

Melt ¼ cup butter or margarine in a pan. Stir in the flour with a wooden spoon and cook gently for 1–2 minutes until the mixture forms a soft ball, stirring constantly.

Remove pan from heat and gradually stir in the 1¼ cups liquid, beating vigorously all the time to obtain a smooth sauce. When all the liquid is incorporated, return pan to heat and bring to the boil, stirring constantly.

Lower the heat and simmer gently until the sauce thickens. Remove pan from the heat. Add the grated cheese and pepper to taste. Stir constantly until the cheese melts. Stir in the chopped clams.

Set the oven at 350°F. Fill the reserved shells (using both halves of each one) with the sauce mixture. If there is any left over, then spoon into a large scallop shell or small ovenproof serving dish.

Mix together the breadcrumbs, grated Parmesan cheese, chives and parsley. Sprinkle over the clams then dot with the remaining butter or margarine.

Put the clams in a single layer in a baking pan and bake in preset oven for 15 minutes or until golden brown.

Transfer to warmed individual serving plates and serve any extra sauce mixture separately.

Deep Fried Sardines

12 fresh sardines
2–3 eggs
salt and pepper
flour for coating
1–1¼ cups fine dry breadcrumbs
oil for deep fat frying

To garnish
few sprigs of parsley
few slices of lemon

Cut the heads and tails off the sardines and split lengthwise under the belly. Clean, then wash thoroughly under cold running water, then pat dry with absorbent paper. Set aside.

Beat the eggs lightly to mix and add salt and pepper to taste. Coat the sardines with flour, then with the egg, and finally in breadcrumbs, making sure that the coating so that they will fry evenly. Press the crumbs on well. Chill in the refrigerator for at least 30 minutes before frying.

Meanwhile, heat the oil in a deep fat fryer until it is hot enough to turn a stale bread cube golden in 20–30 seconds.

Put 1 or 2 sardines in the hot oil and deep fry until golden, turning them gently during cooking. Remove from pan with tongs or a slotted spoon and drain on absorbent paper. Keep hot in the oven on a warmed serving platter while frying remainder.

Serve immediately on individual serving plates, with a garnish of parsley sprigs and lemon slices.

Duchess Potato Mixture

Basic Recipe ☆

1¼ lb old potatoes
1 egg yolk
2 tbsp butter or margarine
¼ tsp grated nutmeg
salt and pepper

Peel potatoes, cut into pieces the same size. Steam for 15–20 minutes until tender. Drain, then rub through a wire sieve to make a smooth paste.

Put into a pan and heat gently until dry, stirring constantly. Beat in remaining ingredients. Pipe while still hot. Then reheat or serve immediately.

Clams Mornay.

Goujons of Sole in Potato Nests.

Goujons of Sole in Potato Nests

Filleted dab may be substituted for the sole if wished. For a more simple starter, the goujons may be served without their potato nests. You will need special frying baskets or 'nids' for the potato nests – available from specialist kitchen shops. Serve with tartare sauce.

3–4 fillets of gray or lemon sole
  or flounder
1–2 eggs
salt and pepper
flour for coating
about 1 cup fine dry breadcrumbs
6–8 medium potatoes
oil for deep fat frying

To garnish
sprigs of parsley
2 lemons

Skin the fish and cut into narrow strips about 2 inches long. Beat the eggs lightly and add salt and pepper to taste. Coat the fish with flour, then with the egg and finally the breadcrumbs making sure the coating is complete so they will fry evenly. Press the crumbs on well. Chill in the refrigerator for at least 30 minute before frying.

Meanwhile, make the potato nests. Peel the potatoes and slice finely on a mandoline, using the fluted blade and criss-crossing the slices to form a waffle pattern. Heat the oil in a deep fat fryer until it is hot enough to turn a stale bread cube golden in 20–30 seconds.

Heat a pair of frying baskets (nids) in the oil. Leave the small basket in the oil and line the larger one with a few waffled potatoes. Place small basket inside large basket and lower into hot oil. Fry until potatoes are golden brown, then remove from fryer. Take out small basket and gently tip out potato nest onto absorbent paper. Drain and keep hot.

Put a few goujons into the hot oil and deep fry until golden, turning them gently during cooking. Remove from pan with a slotted spoon and drain on absorbent paper. Keep hot in the oven while frying remainder.

Pile goujons into potato nests and arrange on a warmed serving platter. Garnish with parsley and wedges of lemon.

Hot appetizers

Coquilles St. Jacques with Duchess Potatoes.

Coquilles St. Jacques

6 scallops
1¼ cups basic fish stock
about ⅔ cup white wine or apple cider
¼ cup butter or margarine
¼ cup + 1 tbsp flour
salt and pepper
1 small onion
1½ cups mushrooms

To finish
basic Duchess potato mixture

Remove scallops from shells. Scrub shells and set aside. Put scallops in a pan with fish stock and poach gently for 5–7 minutes or until tender. Do not boil or this will make scallops tough. Remove from pan and cut into bite sized pieces. Keep hot.

Strain the cooking liquid into a measuring jug and make up to 2 cups with wine or cider. Set aside.

Melt threequarters of the butter or margarine in a pan. Stir in the flour with a wooden spoon and cook gently for 1–2 minutes until the mixture forms a soft ball.

Remove pan from heat and gradually stir in the measured liquid, beating vigorously all the time to obtain a smooth sauce. When all the liquid is incorporated, return pan to heat and bring to the boil, stirring constantly. Lower the heat, add salt and pepper to taste and simmer gently until the sauce is thick and smooth, stirring constantly. Keep hot.

Peel the onion and chop finely. Wipe the mushrooms clean with a damp cloth, but do not peel. Chop finely. Melt the remaining butter or margarine in a skillet, add the onion and fry gently for about 5 minutes until lightly colored. Add the mushrooms to the pan and fry for a further 2 minutes, stirring occasionally.

Remove from heat and stir onion and mushrooms into sauce. Add the scallops and parsley. Taste for seasoning.

Spoon sauce into cleaned scallop shells. Pipe Duchess potato mixture in a border around each scallop shell. Brown under a preheated hot broiler.

Scallops Mornay garnished with parsley.

Scallops Mornay

6 scallops
1¼ cups dry white wine
1 strip of lemon peel
1 bay leaf
6 black peppercorns
about ⅔ cup milk
3 tbsp butter or margarine
¼ cup + 1 tbsp flour
½ cup grated Gruyère or Emmenthaler cheese
¼ tsp ground mace
pepper

To serve
basic Duchess potato mixture
¼ cup grated Parmesan cheese
sprigs of fresh parsley

Remove scallops from shells. Scrub shells and set aside. Put scallops in a pan with the wine, lemon peel, crushed bay leaf and peppercorns, and a little salt. Simmer gently for 5–10 minutes or until tender. Do not boil or this will make scallops tough. Remove from pan and cut into bite sized pieces. Set aside.

Strain the cooking liquid into a measuring jug and make up to 2 cups with milk. Set aside.

Melt the butter or margarine in a pan. Stir in the flour with a wooden spoon and cook gently for 1–2 minutes until the mixture forms a soft ball, stirring constantly.

Remove pan from heat and gradually stir in the measured liquid, beating vigorously all the time to obtain a smooth sauce. When all the liquid is incorporated, return pan to heat and bring to the boil, stirring constantly.

Lower the heat and simmer gently until the sauce is thick and smooth. Remove pan from the heat. Add the grated Swiss cheese with the mace and pepper to taste. Stir constantly until the cheese melts. Stir in scallops. Taste for seasoning.

Set the oven at 400°F. Spoon sauce into cleaned scallop shells. Pipe Duchess potato mixture in a border around each scallop shell. Sprinkle the sauce with grated Parmesan cheese. Stand shells on a cookie sheet and bake in preset oven for 10 minutes or until the potatoes are browned. Garnish with parsley.

Crab Soufflé

1 × 1 lb cooked crab
peel and juice of ½ lemon
4 black peppercorns
1 sprig of fresh parsley
1 bay leaf
3 tbsp butter or margarine
¼ cup brandy
¼ cup dry white wine
cayenne pepper
salt
4 tbsp heavy cream
3 egg yolks
4 egg whites

Remove meat from body and large claws of crab. Clean shell and reserve if required for serving. Crush all other edible parts of the crab and put in a pan with the lemon peel and juice, crushed peppercorns, parsley and bay leaf. Cover with water, bring to the boil and skim. Simmer gently for 20 minutes, then strain and return liquid to rinsed out pan. Boil to reduce to a scant ½ cup.

Melt the butter or margarine in a pan, add the crabmeat and cook gently for a few minutes, stirring occasionally. Warm the brandy in a separate pan, then pour over crab and ignite.

Pour reduced cooking liquid over flames, then pour in the wine. Add cayenne pepper and salt to taste. Whip the cream until thick, then stir into pan. Bring to the boil and cook until thick, stirring occasionally.

Set the oven at 375°F. Transfer mixture to a bowl, leave to cool a little, then beat in the egg yolks. Beat the egg whites until stiff and fold into the crab mixture.

Turn into a buttered 3¾ cup soufflé dish, or 4–6 individual soufflé dishes. If liked, some of the mixture can be piled into the cleaned crab shell.

Bake in the preset oven for about 30 minutes for a large soufflé, 15–20 minutes for soufflés in shell or individual dishes. When risen and golden brown on top, remove from oven and serve immediately.

Fish Stock

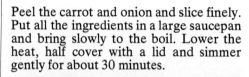

1 carrot
1 onion
1 lb fish trimmings
thinly pared rind and juice
of 1 lemon
1 bay leaf
few sprigs of parsley
few black peppercorns
salt
5 cups water

Peel the carrot and onion and slice finely. Put all the ingredients in a large saucepan and bring slowly to the boil. Lower the heat, half cover with a lid and simmer gently for about 30 minutes.

Remove from heat, cover tightly with a lid. Leave until cold. Strain, then return to rinsed out pan. Boil to reduce to 3¾ cups. Taste for seasoning, then refrigerate until required. Use within 1–2 days.

For a more flavorsome fish stock, use a mixture of water and dry white wine or apple cider rather than just water.

Crab Soufflé.

Hot Creamed Crab

1 × 1 lb cooked crab
1 tsp lemon juice
¼ cup dry sherry
⅜ cup heavy cream
salt and freshly ground black pepper
1 cup fine fresh brown breadcrumbs
5 slices of brown bread
butter or margarine for spreading
  and cooking

To finish
2 tbsp finely chopped parsley

Dress the crab by removing the meat from the body and the large claws. Clean shell and reserve for serving.

Set the oven at 375°F. Mix crabmeat with lemon juice and sherry. Whip the cream until thick, then stir into the crab mixture with salt and pepper to taste. Stir in ⅓ cup breadcrumbs and mix thoroughly. Set aside.

Remove crusts from bread and stamp into 4 inch rounds with a fluted cookie cutter. Spread the rounds with butter and pile the mixture on top and into the cleaned crab shell. Sprinkle tops with remaining breadcrumbs and dot with butter or margarine.

Put the rounds and shell on a cookie sheet and bake in the preset oven for 12–15 minutes until lightly browned. Transfer to a warmed serving platter, sprinkle with parsley and serve immediately.

If preferred, the crab mixture can be baked in individual buttered soufflé or ramekin dishes.

Angels on Horseback

1 pt shucked oysters
½–¾ lb sliced bacon
4–6 slices of bread
watercress

Cut the bacon slices in half and drain the oysters. Wrap each oyster in a piece of bacon and secure it with a cocktail pick or toothpick. Broil the rolls for 2–3 minutes, or until the bacon is crisp.

Remove the crusts from the bread slices. Cut them in squares, toast them and butter.

To serve, remove the picks, arrange the rolls on the slices of toast and garnish with the watercress.

Snails with Garlic Butter with an individual fork and tongs.

Snails with Garlic Butter

Special snail baking dishes are available from specialist kitchen shops. Traditional forks and tongs make it easier to eat the snails.

1 can of snails with shells
1½ cup softened butter
2 cloves of garlic
2 tbsp finely chopped parsley
salt and freshly ground black pepper
rock salt for cooking (if necessary)

Set the oven at 375°F.

Drain off the liquid from the canned snails. Stuff each snail as far as possible down into a shell. Set aside.

Whip the butter with an electric or rotary beater. Peel and crush the garlic, then beat into the butter with the parsley and salt and pepper to taste. Fill each snail shell with garlic butter and level off at the rim.

Stand the snails upright in ovenproof snail dishes or pack a jelly roll pan to the rim with rock salt and push snails into this to hold them firmly upright.

Bake in preset oven on shelf above center for 15 minutes, then serve immediately with hot crusty French bread.

Hot appetizers

Marinated Herrings with a herb stuffing.

Marinated Herrings with Herbs

6 small herrings
1¼ cups wine vinegar and water mixed in
    equal quantities
1 bay leaf
6 black peppercorns
1 small onion
½ tsp salt
6 tbsp melted butter or margarine

For stuffing
1 cup fine fresh white breadcrumbs
2 tbsp finely chopped parsley
2 tbsp chopped chives or scallion tops
1 egg
salt and pepper

To garnish
few slices of lemon
crisply fried potato or onion rings

Ask your fishmonger to clean and bone the herrings for you if you prefer not to do this sort of job yourself. Otherwise, cut the heads and tails off the herrings, then split, clean and bone them. Remove scales. Wash thoroughly under cold running water. Put in a shallow dish with the wine vinegar and water. Crush the bay leaf and peppercorns. Peel and chop the onion finely. Add to the marinade with ½ tsp salt.

Leave to marinate in the refrigerator for 24 hours, spooning the marinade over the herrings from time to time.

The next day, set the oven at 375°F. Mix all the ingredients for the stuffing together, adding salt and pepper to taste. Remove the herrings from the marinade and pat dry with absorbent paper. Fill with the stuffing mixture and reshape. Put herrings in a shallow baking dish and spoon over the melted butter or margarine. Bake in the preset oven for 12–15 minutes until the fish feels just tender when pierced with a skewer.

Meanwhile, boil the marinade in a pan until well reduced. Transfer baked herrings to a warmed serving platter, pour over the marinade and serve hot. Garnish with slices of lemon and crisply fried potato or onion rings, if liked.

If wished, the herrings may be served cold. Prepare up to serving point as above, leave until cool, then chill in the refrigerator before serving.

Grilled Herring Roe on toast.

Grilled Herring Roe

1 lb soft herring roe
flour for coating
salt and pepper
about ½ cup butter or margarine
4 thick slices of white bread
4 large lettuce leaves

To serve
4 lemon wedges (optional)

Wash the roe, drain and pat dry with absorbent paper. Toss in flour seasoned with salt and pepper. Brush the rack of broiler pan with melted butter or margarine and put roe on rack. Brush roe with more melted butter or margarine.

Broil the roe for about 10 minutes, turning them once and brushing with more melted butter or margarine.

Meanwhile, remove crusts from bread and stamp each slice into a 4 inch round with a plain cookie cutter. Toast the rounds and spread with butter or margarine.

Place the toasted rounds on a warmed serving platter and arrange 1 lettuce leaf on each round. Pile broiled roe onto lettuce and sprinkle with salt and pepper. Serve immediately with lemon wedges, if liked.

Pâtés

Pâtés are savory mixtures usually made from chicken, calves' or pigs' liver with the addition of other meat, poultry or game. They can be smooth and velvety or coarse in texture. Serve them as an hors d'oeuvre with cocktails or as an appetizer. Smooth pâtés are served from the dish with a knife or spoon and spread on toast or French bread. Coarse pâtés are often cut in slices. Give each guest a slice or individual pâté and serve the toast and French bread separately.

A terrine is a pâté served in a glazed earthenware casserole, traditionally known as a terrine. They are often more substantial pâtés and can be served as a main dish with a salad accompaniment or as a buffet dish.

The meats for pâtés and terrines should be well seasoned and contain some fat. A little brandy or sherry adds flavor and helps the mixture to keep well. They improve in flavor if they are made two days before serving but they must be sealed with a layer of butter or fat. Store in the refrigerator. They should be served cold but not chilled, so remove from the refrigerator an hour before serving.

Rabbit Pâté served with pickled gherkins and onions.

Rabbit Pâté

1 lb raw rabbit or hare meat
¼ lb raw lean pork or ham
½ lb raw unsalted pork fat
1–2 cloves of garlic, according to taste
1 medium mild onion
6 tbsp dry sherry
1 small egg
salt and pepper
about 8 thin slices of pork
   fat for lining pan

To serve
few sprigs of parsley
hot buttered toast
pickled gherkins and onions (optional)

Any kind of game may be substituted for the rabbit or hare suggested in this recipe. To obtain 1 lb meat, you will need to buy a large animal weighing at least twice this amount.

Set the oven at 350°F. Cut the meats and pork fat into cubes. Peel and crush the garlic. Peel the onion and chop roughly. Grind all these ingredients together, then put in a bowl. Stir in the sherry and egg. Add salt and pepper to taste. Stir well to mix.

Line the base and sides of a 4 cup loaf pan or pâté dish with the slices of pork fat. Spoon in the prepared pâté mixture, pressing it down well with the back of a spoon.

Cover pâté with buttered foil and stand in a roasting pan half filled with hot water. Bake in the preset oven for 1–1½ hours or until the pâté shrinks away from sides of pan or dish, and the juices run faintly pink when pâté is pierced in the center with a skewer.

Remove from roasting pan and leave to cool. Place weights on top of foil and chill in the refrigerator overnight. Turn out onto a heatproof plate or dish. Score the fat in a crisscross pattern and put under a preheated hot broiler until browned.

Leave to cool, then arrange on a serving platter. Garnish around pâté with sprigs of parsley and serve with hot buttered toast and pickled gherkins and onions, if liked.

Pâtés

Rich Chicken Liver Pâté

¾ *lb raw unsalted pork fat*
1 lb chicken livers
2 scallions
1 clove of garlic
2 tbsp dry sherry
2 tbsp brandy
salt and freshly ground black pepper
1 cup sweet butter, softened

To garnish
1 sprig of parsley
⅔ *cup unset basic aspic (optional)*
4 stuffed olives (optional)

Cut ¼ lb pork fat into very thin slivers and put in a heavy based pan. Melt over low heat until fat is runny but not colored. Leave to cool, then chill in the refrigerator until thick but not set. Spread the fat thickly on the base and sides of a deep ovenproof baking dish. Chill in the refrigerator. Meanwhile, cut up the remaining pork fat and chicken livers. Chop the scallions and peel and crush the garlic. Grind all these ingredients together, then put into a bowl. Stir in half the sherry and brandy and salt and pepper to taste. Stir well to mix.

Set the oven at 350°F. Spoon the mixture into the prepared dish, pressing it down well with the back of a spoon. Cover pâté with buttered foil and stand in a roasting pan half filled with hot water. Bake in preset oven for 1 hour, then remove from roasting pan and discard foil. Leave until cold, then chill in the refrigerator. Turn out of baking dish into a fine sieve and rub through into a bowl. Beat in the softened sweet butter. Beat in the remaining sherry and brandy. Taste for seasoning.

Press pâté into a serving bowl or soufflé dish and level the top. Garnish with a sprig of parsley. If preferred, cover the top with half the aspic, arrange sliced stuffed olives over and cover with remaining aspic. Chill in the refrigerator before serving with hot unbuttered toast or melba toast.

This pâté is very smooth and creamy, and because it is rich a little will go a long way.

Two presentations of Rich Chicken Liver Pâté.

Two Layer Pâté garnished with parsley and radishes.

Two Layer Pâté

For first layer
½ lb boned arm steak
½ lb boned stew veal
1 small onion
1 clove of garlic
¾ cup olive oil
¼ cup dry wine, sherry or brandy
1 tbsp dried mixed herbs
¼ tsp grated nutmeg
salt and pepper
¼ lb unsmoked sliced bacon
¼ lb raw unsalted pork fat

For second layer
1 × 2 oz can of anchovies in oil
½ lb pork liver
½ lb unsmoked sliced bacon
3 black peppercorns
2 whole cloves
⅔ cup fine fresh white breadcrumbs
1 egg
¼ cup brandy

To garnish
¼ cup butter
sprigs of parsley
a few radishes

For the first layer: cut the pork and veal into small cubes. Peel the onion and chop finely. Peel and crush the garlic. Put all these ingredients in a bowl with the oil and wine, sherry or brandy, mixed herbs, nutmeg and salt and pepper to taste. Stir well to mix, then leave to marinate in the refrigerator overnight, stirring occasionally.

The next day, drain the mixture in a colander or sieve. Cut the rind off the bacon and discard. Cut the bacon into small pieces with the pork fat. Grind drained meats with the bacon and pork fat. Spread mixture in the bottom of a greased shallow baking dish and set aside.

For the second layer: drain the anchovies and put in a bowl. Cover with milk and leave to soak for at least 30 minutes. Meanwhile, cut the liver into slices. Cut the rind off the bacon and discard. Drain the anchovies and grind with the liver, bacon, peppercorns and cloves. Put in a bowl with the breadcrumbs, egg and brandy and stir well to mix.

Set the oven at 350°F. Spread the second layer of pâté on top of the first and level the top. Cover with buttered foil and stand in a roasting pan half filled with hot water. Bake in preset oven for 1½–2 hours or until the juices run faintly pink when pâté is pierced in the center with a skewer.

Remove from roasting pan and discard foil. Melt the butter in a pan, then pour over the top of pâté. Leave until cold, then chill in the refrigerator. Garnish the top of the pâté with sprigs of parsley and radish roses.

Serve straight from the dish with hot buttered toast or rye bread and butter. This will keep for up to 1 week.

Potted Pork

Potted pork is a simple pâté, usually served in one large dish rather than in individual pots.

2 lb raw unsalted pork fat
2 lb boned blade steak of pork
1¼ cups water
¼ tsp cayenne pepper
salt and pepper

Set the oven at 300°F.

Cut a few thin slices off the pork fat and use to line a deep earthenware baking dish. Dice the remaining fat finely with the boned pork and put into the dish. Add the water, cayenne pepper and salt and pepper to taste. Cover with a lid.

Bake in the preset oven on bottom shelf for 4 hours, stirring the mixture once every hour. After 3 hours of baking, spoon off about ⅓ cups of fat and set aside.

Transfer mixture to a bowl and work to a rough pâté with the back of a spoon. Taste for seasoning. Pack tightly into a deep serving dish (a soufflé dish is ideal) and pour the reserved fat over the top. Leave until cold, then chill in the refrigerator until required, or keep for up to 1 week. Serve with hot toast.

Pâtés

Fine Liver Pâté

1 lb pork liver
milk
½ lb raw unsalted pork fat
1–2 cloves of garlic, according to taste
6 tbsp Madeira, port or full bodied red wine
⅔ cup fine fresh brown breadcrumbs
2 eggs
½ tsp grated nutmeg
salt and pepper
about 8 thin slices of pork fat for lining dish

To serve
hot buttered toast

Set the oven at 350°F.

Cut the liver into slices, put in a bowl and cover with milk. Leave for at least 30 minutes.

Drain the liver and grind with three-quarters of the pork fat. Put into a bowl. Peel and crush the garlic and add to the ground mixture with the Madeira, port or wine, breadcrumbs, eggs, nutmeg and salt and pepper to taste. Stir well to mix. Work the mixture in an electric blender until fine, or strain through a sieve.

Line the base and sides of a deep oven-proof dish with the slices of pork fat. Spoon in the prepared pâté mixture, pressing it down well with the back of a spoon.

Cover pâté with buttered foil and stand in a roasting pan half filled with hot water. Bake in the preset oven for 1–1½ hours or until the pâté shrinks away from sides of dish, and the juices run faintly pink when pâté is pierced in the center with a skewer.

Remove from roasting pan and discard foil. Cut remaining pork fat into very thin slivers and put in a heavy based pan. Melt over low heat until fat is runny but not colored. Pour over pâté in dish, leave until cold, then chill in the refrigerator overnight. Serve from the dish with hot buttered toast.

Make Rillettes de Porc in individual portions for your guests.

Rillettes de Porc

¾ lb raw unsalted pork fat
2 lb boned blade steak of pork
1 clove of garlic
½ cup water
½ tsp dried sage
salt and pepper

Set the oven at 275°F.

Cut the pork fat into thin strips. Dice the pork shoulder finely. Peel and crush the garlic.

Put all the ingredients in an earthenware casserole and cover with a lid. Bake in the preset oven for 4–5 hours until the meat is tender, stirring occasionally.

Transfer the meat to a fine wire sieve placed over a bowl and leave until the fat has strained through. Pound the meat on a board or shred finely with two forks. Taste for seasoning.

Pack the meat into individual earthenware pots or ramekins, pressing it down well with a spoon. Pour the strained fat over the top of each one and leave until cold. Chill in the refrigerator until required, or keep for up to 1 week. Serve with triangles of hot toast.

This is a coarse textured pâté with a fairly high proportion of fat and is therefore relatively inexpensive to make.

Hot Water Crust Pastry

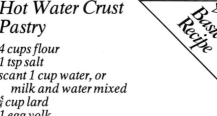

4 cups flour
1 tsp salt
scant 1 cup water, or
    milk and water mixed
⅝ cup lard
1 egg yolk

Sift flour and salt into a warm mixing bowl and make a well in the center. Put the water, or milk and water, in a pan with the lard and bring slowly to the boil, stirring with a wooden spoon until the lard melts.

Put the egg yolk into a well in the center of the flour and pour in the boiling liquid. Beat flour and liquid together with a wooden spoon until a soft dough is formed.

Turn dough out onto a floured board and knead with the hands until smooth. Wrap in a cloth to keep pliable until ready to use. Keep warm.

Use for making raised savory pies, particularly game, pork and veal pies, and pâté en croûte. Hot water crust pastry is usually served cold.

Bacon Pâté

1 lb sliced bacon
1 lb ground pork
1 small onion, finely chopped
2 cups fresh white breadcrumbs
2 hardcooked eggs, chopped
pinch of ground mace
2 eggs, beaten to mix
salt and pepper

Line a loaf pan with 4–5 slices of the bacon. Reserve 6–8 slices and grind or finely chop the rest. Mix this with the pork, onion, breadcrumbs, hardcooked eggs and mace. Stir in the beaten eggs to bind the mixture and season. Mix.

Press a layer of the mixture into the loaf pan and smooth the top. Cover with 3–4 slices of bacon, then press in another layer of the meat mixture. Cover with the remaining bacon and fill up with the meat mixture. Smooth the top and cover with foil.

Set the oven at 325°F. Place the pan in a roasting pan filled with boiling water and bake in the pre set oven for 1¼–1½ hours, or until the pâté is firm to the touch. Remove from the oven, top with a small plate and a light weight and leave to cool.

Pâté en Croûte

This is an unusual recipe as the case for the pâté is made with hot water crust pastry, rather than with the more usual puff pastry.

1½ batches of basic hot water crust pastry
1 batch of uncooked rabbit pâté
2 hardcooked eggs
¼ lb boiled ham

For glaze
1 egg
1 tsp oil
¼ tsp salt
¼ tsp pepper

To garnish
few parsley sprigs

Set the oven at 325°F.

Put threequarters of the pastry in the center of a 9 inch hinged pie mold placed on a warmed cookie sheet. Push with the fingertips, gradually working the dough up the sides of the mold. Cut off trimmings, add to remaining quarter of dough and wrap in a cloth to keep pliable. Keep warm.

Divide the pâté in two and press one half into the bottom of the lined mold. Arrange the hardcooked eggs lengthwise, pushing them down into the pâté. Cut the ham into thin strips and place over the eggs. Press the remaining pâté into the mold.

Fold the top edge of the pastry over the pâté and brush with a little water. Roll out the reserved pastry to a shape for the lid and press into position. Use any trimmings to decorate the top, if liked.

Bake in the preset oven for 1 hour. Meanwhile, beat together the ingredients for the glaze, then strain. Remove mold from oven and brush pastry with the glaze. Return to oven and cook for a further 1½–2 hours until the pastry is crisp and golden brown.

Remove from oven, leave to rest for 5 minutes, then remove the mold, leaving the pâté on the cookie sheet. Leave until cold, then garnish with parsley.

Pâté en Croute.

Chicken or Duck Pâté and Pâté Maison with identical garnishes and Pâté in Fried Bread.

Terrine of Chicken

3 lb ready-to-cook broiler-fryer chicken
½ lb boned stew veal
½ lb boned blade steak of pork
1 lb unsmoked bacon slices
⅔ cup port or full bodied red wine
2 tbsp brandy
finely grated rind and juice of 1 lemon
1 egg
1 tsp powdered allspice
½ tsp powdered mace
salt and pepper

To finish (optional)
⅔ cup unset basic aspic
few stuffed olives
baby pickled onions

Skin and bone the chicken. Cut the breast meat into thin slivers and set aside. Cut the remaining chicken into small pieces with the veal and pork. Cut the rind off the bacon and discard. Chop half the bacon roughly, reserving half the slices for the center of terrine.

Grind the small pieces of chicken, veal, pork and bacon. Put in a bowl, add the port or wine, brandy, lemon rind and juice, egg, allspice and mace. Season to taste with salt and pepper and stir well to mix.

Set the oven at 350°F. Put half the ground mixture into the bottom of a buttered terrine or baking pan and press down well with a spoon. Arrange half the reserved bacon slices on top, then the reserved chicken breast meat. Cover with remaining bacon slices and spoon in the remaining minced mixture.

Cover with buttered foil or a lid and stand in a roasting pan half filled with hot water. Bake in the preset oven for about 1½ hours or until the juices run faintly pink when terrine is pierced in the center with a skewer. Remove from roasting pan and leave to cool. Place weights on top of foil and chill in the refrigerator overnight. Serve straight from the terrine, decorated with aspic, stuffed olives and baby pickled onions, if liked. Serve hot buttered toast separately.

If liked, duck may be substituted for the chicken. In this case, the lemon rind and juice should be omitted and orange used instead.

Pâté Maison

1 lb unsalted pork fat
1×2 oz cans of anchovies in oil
milk
1 medium onion
1 lb pork liver
½ lb boned arm steak of pork
¼ lb ground beef
3 eggs
¼ cup flour
⅔ cup light cream
½ tsp powdered mace
½ tsp grated nutmeg
pepper

To garnish (optional)
few slices of cucumber
few tomatoes

If a coarse textured pâté is preferred, then do not blend the mixture before baking. For a milder flavor, calf's or lamb's liver may be substituted for pork liver.

Cut a few thin slices off the pork fat and use to line a 4 cup baking pan, terrine or loaf pan. Set aside. Drain the anchovies and put in a bowl. Cover with milk and leave to soak for at least 30 minutes.

Meanwhile, peel the onion and chop finely. Grind with the liver, pork and remaining fat. Drain the anchovies, chop roughly and add to the ground mixture with the beef. Stir well to mix, then work in an electric blender until smooth.

Set the oven at 350°F. Put the eggs in a bowl and gradually stir in the flour and cream. Beat well to mix, then beat into the ground meat mixture with the seasonings.

Spoon into prepared dish or pan, pressing down well and smoothing the top. Cover with buttered foil or a lid and stand in a roasting pan half filled with hot water. Bake in the preset oven for about 1½ hours or until the pâté shrinks away from sides of dish or pan and the juices run faintly pink when pâté is pierced in the center with a skewer.

Remove from roasting pan and leave to cool. Place weights on top of foil and chill in the refrigerator overnight. Turn out onto a serving platter and garnish with slices of cucumber and tomato, or leave in dish and decorate with aspic, stuffed olives and baby pickled onions. Serve hot buttered toast separately.

Pâté in Fried Bread

Pâté and cheese sauce in a cube of fried bread makes a substantial starter for a dinner party, or a filling snack or supper meal when served with a mixed salad. Allow one slice per person.

oil for deep fat frying
2 slices of white bread
    about 4 inches thick
milk
¼ lb homemade or bought liver pâté
1¼ cups hot basic Mornay sauce
½ cup grated Cheddar cheese
cayenne pepper

To garnish
few sprigs of parsley

Melt the oil in a deep fat fryer until it is hot enough to turn a stale bread cube golden in 20–30 seconds.

Cut the crusts off the bread and hollow out the insides, leaving about ¼ inch around the base and sides to make a container for the filling. Dip the bread in milk.

Put one bread square in the fryer and deep fry until it is golden brown, turning the bread over until it is cooked on all sides. Lift out with tongs, drain on absorbent paper and keep hot in the oven while frying the second square of bread. Spoon the pâté into the fried bread, dividing it equally between them. Spoon in the prepared Mornay sauce and keep hot. Sprinkle the grated cheese and 2 dashes of cayenne pepper. Put the squares under a preheated hot broiler until browned on top. Transfer to individual serving plates and garnish with parsley sprigs. Serve immediately.

Pâtés

Chicken Liver Pâté

This pâté is quick to make because it is fried on top of the stove rather than baked in the oven.

1 small onion
1 clove of garlic
salt
6 tbsp butter
¼ lb chicken livers
1 tsp dried mixed herbs
2 tbsp brandy
freshly ground black pepper

To finish
6 tbsp melted butter
¼ tsp cayenne pepper
1–2 tbsp finely chopped parsley

Peel the onion and chop finely. Peel the garlic and crush with ½ tsp salt. Melt 4 tbsp butter in a pan, add the onion and garlic and fry gently for about 5 minutes until lightly colored.

Meanwhile, chop the chicken livers roughly. Add to the pan and cook gently for 10 minutes, stirring occasionally until evenly browned. Remove from heat and leave to cool a little. Work mixture in an electric blender until smooth, or strain through a sieve. Beat in the remaining butter, the mixed herbs, brandy and salt and pepper to taste.

Spoon the pâté into a serving dish and press down well. Pour melted butter over the top and chill in the refrigerator until set. Sprinkle with cayenne pepper and parsley before serving with black bread and pickled gherkins.

Farmhouse Pâté

A combination of marinated meats and pork fat, Farmhouse Pâté looks very attractive when served showing the different smooth and coarse layers.

½ boned raw hare or rabbit
½ lb boneless stew veal
¼ lb boiled ham
1¼ lb raw unsalted pork fat
1 medium onion
1 clove of garlic
4 black peppercorns
1 bay leaf
½ cup dry red wine
1 tbsp finely chopped parsley
salt
2 eggs
2 tbsp brandy (optional)

To seal
flour
water

Cut the hare or rabbit, veal, ham and half the pork fat into very thin strips. Peel the onion and chop finely. Peel and crush the garlic. Crush the peppercorns and bay leaf. Put all these ingredients in a bowl with the wine, parsley and salt and stir well to mix. Cover and leave to marinate in the refrigerator for 24 hours, stirring from time to time.

The next day, grind half the mixture finely, or work in an electric blender until smooth. Beat in the eggs and brandy. Cut the remaining pork fat into thin slices and use threequarters to line the base and sides of a large terrine or baking pan with a lid.

Set the oven at 350°F. Spoon one third of the ground mixture into the bottom of the dish, pressing it down well. Cover with a layer of half the marinated strips. Repeat these 2 layers once more and finish with another ground layer. Cover with the remaining fat, then with buttered foil. Put lid on dish and seal the edge with a thick paste of flour and water to make it airtight.

Stand terrine or dish in a roasting pan half filled with hot water. Bake in preset oven for 2 hours. Remove from roasting pan and cut away crust. Remove lid and leave pâté to cool. Place weights on top of foil and chill in the refrigerator overnight.

Serve straight from the baking pan, or stamp out circles of cold pâté with a small cookie cutter and arrange on a serving platter with softened pâté piped on top.

Rounds of Farmhouse Pâté with pâté rosettes and Chicken Liver Pâté.

Simple Raised Pie

1½ batches of basic hot water crust pastry
½ lb chicken livers
2 tbsp butter
1½ lb finely ground lean pork
2 tbsp port or sherry
2 tbsp brandy
2 eggs
1 tsp dried tarragon
salt and pepper

For glaze
1 egg
1 tsp oil
½ tsp salt
½ tsp pepper

Set the oven at 325°F.

Put threequarters of the pastry in center of a 9 inch hinged pie mold placed on a warmed cookie sheet. Push with the fingertips, gradually working the pastry up the sides of the mold. Cut off trimmings, add to remaining quarter of the pastry and wrap in a cloth. Keep warm.

Cut the chicken livers into small pieces and fry in hot butter until browned on all sides. Remove from pan with a slotted spoon and mix into the ground pork with the remaining ingredients.

Press mixture into the mold. Fold the top edge of the pastry over the pâté and brush with a little water. Roll out the reserved pastry to a shape for the lid and press into position. Use any trimmings to decorate the top, if liked.

Bake in the preset oven for 1 hour. Meanwhile, beat together the ingredients for the glaze, then strain. Remove mold from oven and brush pastry with the glaze. Return to oven and cook for a further 1¾ hours until the pastry is crisp and golden.

Remove from oven, leave to rest for 5 minutes, then remove the mold, leaving the pâté on the cookie sheet. Serve cold.

Simple Raised Pie garnished with parsley and Terrine of Pork.

Terrine of Pork

1 lb pork liver
milk
¾ lb boned blade steak of pork
1 small onion
1 tbsp flour
2 eggs
2 tbsp brandy
2 tbsp fine fresh white breadcrumbs
6 juniper berries
1 tsp finely chopped fresh sage, or
    ½ tsp dried sage
salt and pepper
½ lb raw unsalted pork fat or bacon slices

Cut the liver into slices, put in a bowl and cover with milk. Leave for at least 30 minutes. Cut the pork into small pieces. Peel the onion and chop finely. Drain the liver. Grind all these ingredients twice to obtain a very fine mixture.

Put in a bowl with the flour, eggs, brandy and breadcrumbs and beat well to mix. Crush the juniper berries finely and stir into the mixture with the sage and salt and pepper to taste.

Set the oven at 350°F. Cut the pork fat into thin slices. If using bacon, cut off the rind and stretch the bacon with the blade of a sharp knife. Line the base and sides of a 4 cup ovenproof terrine or baking pan with threequarters of the fat or bacon. Spoon in the prepared pâté and press down well. Cover with remaining fat or bacon, then with buttered foil.

Stand terrine or pan in a roasting pan half filled with hot water. Bake in the preset oven for about 1½ hours or until the pâté shrinks away from sides of dish and the juices run faintly pink when the pâté is pierced in the center with a skewer.

Remove from roasting pan and leave to cool. Place weights on top of foil and chill in the refrigerator overnight.

Pâtés

Smoked Trout Pâté

2 smoked trout
2 slices of white bread
a little milk
½ an 8 oz package cream cheese
1 tsp anchovy flavoring
juice of ½ lemon
freshly ground black pepper

To serve
1 bunch watercress
butter
1 long French loaf

Remove crusts from bread and discard. Soak bread in a little milk for about 5 minutes, then squeeze dry. Put in a bowl with the cream cheese, anchovy flavoring, lemon juice and pepper to taste. Beat well to mix.

Remove skin and bones from trout and discard. Put trout flesh in a mortar or bowl and pound to a paste with a pestle or kitchen mallet. Beat into the cream cheese mixture until thoroughly combined. Taste for seasoning. Spoon mixture into a serving dish or press into a 2½ cup oiled mold. Smooth the top. Chill in the refrigerator for 24 hours.

The next day, unmold the pâté on a serving platter if chilled in a mold, or serve straight from the dish. Garnish with watercress and serve with chunks of hot buttered French bread.

Five Minute Pâté

6 oz chicken livers
2 shallots
2–3 cloves of garlic
2 tbsp brandy
1 tbsp light cream
½ tbsp soft margarine
1 tbsp butter

Chop the chicken livers and season with salt and pepper. Crush the garlic and finely chop the shallots.

Melt the margarine in a skillet and gently cook the garlic and shallots until soft. Add the chicken livers and cook over a low heat for about 3 minutes, mashing them with a wooden spoon. Turn off the heat and continue to mash the mixture until smooth. Stir in the cream and then turn the mixture into a serving bowl.

Melt the butter and pour over the pâté to seal. Chill before serving.

Fish Roe Pâté garnished with black olives.

Kippered Herring Pâté

1 lb kippered herring fillets
½ cup butter, softened
2 slices of white bread
a little milk
freshly ground black pepper

To garnish (optional)
few rolled anchovy fillets
few black olives
few shrimps

Brush the kippered herrings with a little butter. Cook under a preheated hot broiler for about 5 minutes, then turn over, brush with a little more butter and broil for a further 5 minutes. Remove from broiler and leave to cool a little.

Chilled Smoked Trout Pâté served with hot French bread.

pinch of allspice, herbs and salt and pepper.

Purée the mixture, a little at a time, in a blender or beat together thoroughly.

Line a medium loaf pan with bacon slices, fill with the mixture and press down well. Smooth the top, cover with foil and place in a roasting pan filled with boiling water. Bake in the preset oven for 1–1¼ hours or until the pâté is firm to the touch.

Cool the pâté until it is tepid, then cover with wax paper, press it into the pan with a board and a light weight and leave until cold. Turn out and serve cut in slices, or cover with melted butter and refrigerate until required.

Fish Roe Pâté

¼ lb smoked cod's roe
¼ lb soft herring roe
2 slices white bread
water
⅔ cup corn oil
juice of 1–2 lemons
cayenne pepper

To finish
few black olives
⅔ cup unset basic aspic

Skin the smoked cod's roe. Fry the soft herring roe in a little of the oil for 7–10 minutes. Meanwhile, remove crusts from bread and discard. Soak bread in a little water for about 5 minutes, then squeeze dry and put in a mortar or bowl.

Remove roe from pan, leave to cool a little, then put in mortar with the smoked roe. Pound the mixture with a pestle or kitchen mallet until smooth and well mixed. Add the oil a drop at a time, beating vigorously after each addition until the mixture becomes thick. Beat in lemon juice and cayenne pepper to taste.

Spoon the pâté into a serving dish, smooth the top and sprinkle with a little cayenne pepper. If liked, the pâté may be decorated with a few strips of pitted black olive and coated in aspic. Chill in the refrigerator until serving time. Serve with hot buttered toast.

Meanwhile, remove crusts from bread and discard. Soak bread in a little milk for about 5 minutes, then squeeze dry and put in a mortar or bowl. Remove skin and bones from kippered herrings and discard. Put flesh in the mortar with the remaining butter and plenty of black pepper. Pound the mixture with a pestle or kitchen mallet until a smooth paste is formed.

Transfer pâté to a serving bowl or individual dishes, smooth the top and mark with the prongs of a fork. Garnish with anchovies, olives and shrimps, if liked. Serve with hot toast.

Pâté de Campagne

1 lb ground veal or pork
½ lb pigs' liver, ground
¼ lb pork fat, ground
6–8 bacon slices
1 shallot, finely chopped
5 slices firm white bread, crusts removed
¼ cup port
3 eggs, beaten
allspice
1 tsp thyme or marjoram
salt and pepper

Set the oven at 350°F.

Combine the ground meat, liver, pork fat and shallot in a bowl. Soak the bread in port and add to the meat with the eggs, a

Sardine Pâté

2 × 7 oz cans sardines in oil
4 hardcooked eggs
about 3 tbsp basic lemon mayonnaise
1 tbsp Worcestershire sauce
¼ cup heavy cream
pepper

To finish (optional)
few sprigs of fresh fennel
⅔ cup unset basic aspic

Drain the sardines, cut off the tails and remove all bones and scales. Mash flesh with a fork. Sieve the eggs and mix into the sardines with the mayonnaise and Worcestershire sauce. Beat until thoroughly combined.

Whip the cream until thick and fold into the sardine mixture. Add pepper to taste. Spoon pâté into a serving bowl and smooth the top. Arrange fennel sprigs in a decorative pattern and spoon over the aspic. Chill in the refrigerator until set. Serve with hot buttered toast.

Lemon Mayonnaise

Basic Recipe

2 egg yolks
½ tsp ready prepared French mustard
salt
½ tsp crushed black peppercorns
1 cup olive or corn oil
juice of 1 lemon

To finish
1 lemon
1 tbsp fresh single cream

Put the egg yolks, mustard, salt and pepper in a bowl. Beat with a wooden spoon, electric or rotary beater until well mixed. Add the oil a drop at a time, beating well after each addition until the mayonnaise begins to thicken.

When half the oil is incorporated, beat in half the lemon juice. Continue adding the oil in a steady stream, then beat in the remaining lemon juice. Taste for seasoning, then cover and store in a cool place until required.

Cut the peel, pith and skin away from the lemon by cutting from the top and working in a spiral down to the bottom, using a sawing motion. Cut the lemon into segments, then chop into small pieces.

Discard all pips, pith and central core. Stir lemon pieces into the mayonnaise with the cream just before serving.

Taramasalata

1 thick slice of white bread
milk
¼ lb smoked cod's roe
½ cup olive oil
1 clove of garlic
1 tbsp finely grated onion
juice of 1 lemon
freshly ground black pepper

To finish
2 tbsp finely chopped parsley
2–3 black olives

Remove crusts from bread and discard. Soak bread in a little milk for about 5 minutes. Meanwhile, skin the cod's roe and pound to a paste in a mortar with a pestle. Squeeze the bread dry and gradually work into the roe.

Add the oil a drop at a time, beating vigorously after each addition until the mixture becomes thick. Peel and crush the garlic and add to the taramasalata with the grated onion, lemon juice and black pepper to taste. Beat until thoroughly combined.

Transfer taramasalata to a serving bowl and smooth the top. Decorate the top with chopped parsley and halved, stoned black olives. Chill in the refrigerator until serving time. Serve with hot pitta bread (flat Greek bread) or toast.

Shrimp Cream

¾ lb fresh shrimps
⅜ cup olive or corn oil
juice of ½ lemon
¼–½ tsp cayenne pepper
salt
⅔ cup heavy cream

If you do not have an electric blender, then you can make this pâté by straining the mixture through a fine sieve. Prawns may be substituted for the shrimps.

Chop the shrimps roughly, reserving a few whole ones for the garnish. Put in an electric blender with the oil, lemon juice, cayenne pepper and salt to taste. Purée until smooth.

Whip the cream until thick. Fold into the shrimp mixture until evenly mixed. Taste for seasoning.

Spoon into a serving bowl and smooth the top. Decorate with reserved whole shrimps and sprinkle with a little cayenne. Chill in the refrigerator until firm. Serve with fingers of hot buttered toast.

Swiss Kippered Toasts

4 kippered herring fillets
butter or margarine
¼ cup cream cheese
¼ cup light cream
juice of ½ lemon
freshly ground black pepper
4 slices brown or wholemeal bread
¼ lb Gruyère or Emmenthaler cheese

To garnish
a few sprigs of watercress

Brush the kippered herrings with a little butter or margarine. Cook under a preheated hot broiler for about 5 minutes, then turn over, brush with a little more butter or margarine and broil for a further 5 minutes. Remove from broiler and leave to cool a little.

Remove skin and bones and discard. Put flesh in a mortar or bowl and pound to a paste with a pestle or kitchen mallet. Add the cream cheese, cream, lemon juice and plenty of black pepper. Beat mixture until thoroughly combined.

Toast the bread and spread with butter or margarine. Pile fish and cheese mixture on top of each slice and place in individual heatproof serving dishes. Slice the Gruyère or Emmenthaler very thinly and place on top. Dot with a little butter or margarine.

Cook under a preheated hot broiler for about 5 minutes until the cheese bubbles and browns. Garnish each plate with a sprig of watercress and serve hot. Allow one slice per person.

If liked, these toasts can be made with Kippered Herring Pâté.

Swiss Kippered Toasts are a delicious snack.

Salads and snacks

Colorful and well-presented salads are one of the simplest and most versatile dishes. Serve them as a starter, a side dish or a main course.

A salad starter, especially on summer days will refresh the appetite for the courses to follow. A side salad will provide a welcome astringency of flavor. Main course or more substantial salads are perfect for lunches or suppers.

Salads can often be prepared in advance, only requiring the addition of a dressing at the last minute. Ingredients can be fresh, canned, or frozen, and can be a useful way of using leftovers. Texture and color are important. Choose contrasting colors. Cooked vegetables should be firm not mushy and crisp vegetables should be really crisp. Cold weather shouldn't mean the end of salads. Combine potatoes and apples with winter vegetables for a more varied diet.

To have a continual variety of snacks is often difficult for the family cook. We give some ideas for interesting snacks, many of which could be served with a side salad.

Potato Salad with Garlic.

Potato Salad with Garlic

3 lb potatoes
1 large clove of garlic
1–2 tsp Dijon mustard
$\frac{1}{8}$ cup white wine vinegar
$\frac{3}{8}$ cup salad oil
1 large crust of bread (brown or white)
1 cup stock

For garnish
1 crisp lettuce
paprika
chopped parsley
sliced black olives

Boil or steam potatoes in their skins. Peel garlic clove and cut in half. Make up stock, if none in refrigerator.

Peel potatoes and cut into dice. Rub salad bowl thoroughly (preferably a wooden one for this classic salad) with a cut clove of garlic, then add the mustard and some of the vinegar. Adding oil and vinegar alternately, whisk together until a thick French dressing consistency is achieved and the oil is totally 'absorbed' into the mixture. Crush the rubbed garlic and spread it over the crumb side of the bread crust.

Cut crust into julienne (matchstick) strips and place in salad bowl. Stir with dressing until well coated. Add potatoes and toss. When coated with dressing, bring stock quickly to the boil, and pour over the potatoes. Toss again and leave to cool.

To serve the salad place on a bed of crisp lettuce leaves and garnish with a sprinkling of paprika, chopped parsley and a few black olive slices.

This salad can be turned into a substantial snack by the addition of matchstick thin strips of garlic sausage, salami, or Frankfurters. It is good served with watercress or crisp curly French endive.

Salads and snacks

Tuna Fish Peppers

2 large red bell peppers
scant ¾ cup long grain rice
¼ lb green beans
1 shallot or medium onion
black olives
green olives
¼ lb peas
small can tuna fish
1 tsp chopped fresh thyme, if available,
* or ½ tsp dried thyme*
a little basic mayonnaise
salt and pepper

Cut peppers in halves lengthwise and re-move core and seeds. Cook rice and drain; rinse in cold water, spread out on a cookie sheet or flat dish and leave to dry. Cook green beans – if not from a can – and cut into dice. Peel and grate shallot or onion. Pit and chop olives. Cook peas and drain, if not from a can. Drain and flake tuna fish. Mix together the rice, beans, grated onion, diced olives, peas and fish. When thoroughly mixed, season and bind with mayonnaise and pile into red pepper halves. Sprinkle with thyme and serve.

Extra mayonnaise may be served sepa-rately. Alternatively, bind the salad ingre-dients together with a little French dres-sing and omit the mayonnaise.

Lemon Dressing

1 clove of garlic
½ tsp salt
6 black peppercorns
2 tbsp finely chopped fresh parsley
1¼ cups olive or corn oil
2 lemons

Peel the garlic and crush with salt. Crush the peppercorns. Put in a bowl with the parsley and gradually beat in the oil and the juice of 1 lemon.

Cut the peel, pith and skin away from remaining lemon by cutting from the top and working in a spiral down to the bot-tom, using a sawing motion. Cut the lemon into segments, then chop into very small pieces. Discard all pips, pith and central core.

Stir lemon pieces into the dressing and taste for seasoning. Serve hot as an accom-paniment to rich or oily fish such as her-ring or mackerel, or cold as a dressing for salads. Heat in a pan if to be served hot, or chill in the refrigerator if to be served cold. Beat well before serving.

Green Pepper Salad

¾ lb green bell peppers
1½ lb small ripe tomatoes
½ cup salad oil
1 tbsp wine vinegar
chopped chives and parsley
salt and pepper

Cut peppers in half, scoop out seeds and cut flesh into strips. Slice tomatoes, leav-ing the skins on.

Put peppers and tomatoes in a bowl, sprinkle with salt and pepper, add oil, then vinegar and mix well. Sprinkle chives and parsley over to garnish and adjust season-ing, if necessary.

This simple salad is ideal for serving with a selection of cold meats, or poultry.

Green Pepper Salad.

Tuna Fish Peppers.

Salads and snacks

Trout and Salad served with mayonnaise make a very enjoyable snack.

1. Tuck lobster tail underneath and grasp the lobster firmly around the middle. With a sharp knife, cut firmly through the top part of the head.

2. Turn the lobster around and continue to cut through the rest of the head straight down through the tail.

3. Open out the two halves on a board and remove the dark thread (intestine) running down the tail, and the weed sac found at the top of the head. Leave the coral (eggs) at the sides. The greenish part in the head is the liver – and is a delicacy.

4. Twist off the big claws, crack them and carefully pick out the meat. Twist off the small claws and crack to remove the meat from these with a skewer. Then, remove the rest of the meat for serving according to your recipe.

Lobster Salad.

Trout and Salad

2–3 medium lake trout
cooking oil
1 crisp lettuce heart (from an Iceberg
*   lettuce or romaine)*
1 tomato
1 lemon
a few slices of cucumber
3–4 radishes
chopped parsley
¾–1 cup basic mayonnaise
salt and pepper

Set the oven at 375°F.

Clean the trout, and place each on a large square of kitchen foil. Brush with a little cooking oil, season lightly and wrap up loosely. Place foil parcels on a cookie sheet and bake in the preset oven for 12–15 minutes, or until cooked. Allow to cool.

Separate lettuce leaves, wash and dry. Arrange on a serving dish. Scald and skin the tomato and place slices on the dish. Garnish the sides of the dish with lemon wedges, cucumber slices and radishes, trimmed and cut into flowers, if liked.

Place the cold trout on the bed of lettuce and sprinkle with chopped parsley. Serve mayonnaise separately.

For a summer touch, add a drop or two of green food coloring to the basic mayonnaise.

Lobster Salad

1 medium, cooked lobster
1 lb potatoes
1 crisp lettuce heart (from an Iceberg
*   or romaine lettuce)*
1 cup canned pimiento
¾ lb peas
1 cup thick basic mayonnaise

With a sharp knife, split lobster in half lengthwise. Remove the dark thread (the intestine) and the small sac that contains weed, which is to be found in the top of the head. Crack the claws and extract the meat, removing the membrane that lies down the middle of the claw. Lift out tail meat and reserve tail shell to be used as a garnish. Remove the body meat and dice.

Boil or steam potatoes, peel and cut into dice. Wash and dry lettuce. Cut pimiento into strips. Cook peas and drain, if not from a can.

Mix together diced lobster meat, potatoes, pimiento strips and most of the peas, reserving a few for decoration. Bind with about half the mayonnaise and serve the rest separately. Pile salad into the center of a serving dish and surround with leaves of crisp, washed lettuce. Add the rest of the peas and decorate the salad with lobster claws and tail shell.

Salads and snacks

Cream Cheese and Greengage Salad

8 fresh ripe greengages
¼ cup shelled pecan nuts
half an 8 oz package cream cheese
⅛–¼ cup heavy cream
paprika
heart of a crisp lettuce (Iceberg or romaine)
salt and pepper

Make a cross cut in the top of each greengage and cut back carefully into four petal shaped points. Remove pits. Crush nuts in a mill. Wash and separate leaves from lettuce heart.

Beat the cream cheese with a little cream to a piping consistency, add nuts, blend well into the cheese and season with salt and pepper. Fill a pastry bag with a medium-size star nozzle and pipe a rosette of cream cheese into each greengage. Sprinkle each with a little paprika to garnish and set on a bed of lettuce leaves. Serve chilled with extra green salad on the side. Allow two fruits per person.

Chaudfroid Sauce

Basic Recipe

2 tsp powdered gelatin
4 tbsp water or chicken stock
1 cup unset basic aspic
1½ cups cool basic velouté sauce

Sprinkle the gelatin over the water or stock in a small heatproof bowl and leave until spongy. Stand the bowl in a pan of gently simmering water until gelatin has dissolved. Remove from pan and leave to cool slightly.

Stir cooled gelatin mixture into unset aspic, then beat aspic into cool velouté sauce until evenly distributed. Use immediately to coat food. Leave until set before serving.

Use for coating cold dishes of fish, meat and poultry to give a decorative touch.

Garlic Bread

Basic Recipe

1 long French loaf, or 1 small uncut white loaf
½ cup butter
2 cloves of garlic
salt and freshly ground black pepper

Set the oven at 400°F.

Cut the loaf into thick slices without cutting right through to the base. Set aside.

Beat the butter until soft and light. Peel and crush the garlic, then beat into the butter with salt and pepper to taste.

Spread the butter on the cut surfaces of the bread and reshape the loaf. Wrap tightly in foil. Place directly on oven shelf. Bake for 10 minutes, then open foil at the top and bake for a further 5 minutes until crisp. Remove foil altogether, arrange bread on a warmed serving platter and serve immediately.

As an alternative to garlic, you can make herb bread, substituting 4 tbsp finely chopped fresh herbs for the garlic cloves. Choose parsley, chives or marjoram for a good flavor.

Cream Cheese and Mushroom Salad

½ lb small mushrooms
basic French dressing
lemon juice
chopped parsley
2–3 medium carrots
small bunch watercress
8 oz package cream cheese
2 tbsp light cream or milk, if necessary
celery salt
black pepper

Slice mushrooms neatly and moisten with French dressing and a good squeeze of lemon juice. Chop parsley; peel and cut carrots into julienne (matchstick) strips, or grate them lengthwise. Wash and dry watercress.

Beat cream cheese until smooth, adding 1–2 tbsp cream or milk, if necessary. Season with celery salt and black pepper. Fill into a pastry bag fitted with a star nozzle and pipe a rosette onto each of four plates. Lift the mushroom slices from the French dressing and arrange round the base of the cream cheese. Sprinkle with chopped parsley and chill. Arrange the carrots and

Our Special Russian Salad has been set in a ring

cress in a side dish, and serve with a little extra French dressing, if liked.

This salad is especially good served with Melba toast.

mold and filled with extra vegetables.

Special Russian Salad

A Russian Salad is traditionally made of a mixture of diced cooked vegetables, such as potatoes, peas, white turnips, carrots, green beans or celery, which are bound together with mayonnaise. It is better – and saves both cooking time and scalded fingers – to peel and dice the vegetables before boiling or steaming them. Choose 'waxy' potatoes for preference, as they are less likely to fall apart during cooking. To

fill a 2½ cup ring mold, you will need:

2 medium carrots
2 medium potatoes
1 small white turnip
¼ cup peas
¼ cup green beans
1 stalk celery
¾ cup thick basic mayonnaise
1 tsp gelatin
1 tbsp lemon juice
1 tbsp orange juice

Peel, dice and cook all vegetables, unless from a can. Slice celery and chop finely. Dissolve the gelatin in the lemon juice and orange juice, then add 2 tbsp cold water and whisk into the mayonnaise. Bind the diced vegetables with this and fill an oiled 2½ cup ring mold. Wrap in foil and chill in refrigerator. To serve, turn out of mold and garnish with extra vegetables.

117

Salads and snacks

Mimosa Salad

¼ cup peas
¼ cup green beans
2–3 stalks celery
6–8 scallions
2 medium potatoes
basic mayonnaise to bind

To garnish
6 eggs
1½ cups small mushrooms, chopped
a little salad oil to moisten
½ tomato (optional)

Cook peas and drain, if not from a can; cut green beans into small slices and cook; wash and chop celery; wash scallions and slice, discard tough, dark green stems; cut potatoes into dice and cook. Soak mushrooms in a little oil.

Mix together salad vegetables, adding just enough basic mayonnaise to bind well. Spoon into a bowl and smooth over top. Mark surface into six equal sections, using a knife. Hardcook eggs and remove yolks. Push yolks through a sieve and chop up whites very finely. Sprinkle whites, then yolks, over the top of the salad to decorate, starting from the edge and working to the center. Fill the remaining two sections with the drained, oiled mushrooms and place a tomato in the center of the dish to garnish.

The 'Mimosa' of the title refers to the hardcooked egg yolk garnish. This is a special party version of the dish. Usually, the egg yolks are sprinkled liberally over a green salad mixture.

Iris Salad

1 clove of garlic
½ red bell pepper
½ green bell pepper
6 pitted green olives
6 pitted black olives
2 crisp lettuce hearts (from an Iceberg or romaine)
5 tomatoes
3 eggs
⅝ cup wine vinegar
paprika
⅞ cup salad oil
salt and pepper
1 tbsp sweet pickle
2 bananas

To garnish
flaked almonds

Crush garlic clove with a little salt. Scoop out seeds and core from both peppers, then cut into strips. Chop up olives. Wash lettuce leaves. Skin and slice tomatoes. Hardcook eggs.

In a bowl, pour the vinegar, add the garlic, paprika and oil. Whisk until blended and season with salt and pepper. Add peppers, olives and sweet pickle. Toss until coated thoroughly with dressing. Leave to chill.

On a bed of lettuce leaves, arrange slices of tomato and hardcooked egg. Peel the bananas at the last minute and chop. Add to platter. Garnish with flaked almonds, if liked, and pour over the chilled dressing. Serve with French bread.

Carrot and Walnut Salad

3–4 medium carrots
8 walnuts
¼ cup fresh orange juice
½ cup basic mayonnaise
salt and pepper

Peel carrots and cut into julienne (matchstick) strips. Crack walnuts, cut the flesh into quarters. Beat orange juice into the mayonnaise.

Mix walnuts with carrot sticks in a bowl and season. Spoon over dressing and toss salad just before serving.

About ⅔ cup basic French dressing can be used as an alternative to mayonnaise. Flavor with the grated rind of half an orange, if liked. The carrots can be mixed with julienne strips of celeriac.

Mimosa Salad.

Lazy Daisy Salad for lazy days!

Lazy Daisy Salad

cooked or canned vegetables – cauliflower,
  carrot, green beans, peas
small can asparagus tips
new potatoes
basic French dressing
1 clove of garlic
thick basic mayonnaise

To garnish
1–2 cooked egg whites

This salad is quick to put together, using any cooked leftover, or canned vegetables you have. Boil the potatoes, drain and cool. Dice the vegetables (except asparagus tips) and toss in French dressing.

Cut the garlic clove and rub around the serving dish to flavor. Arrange all the vegetables in the dish except the asparagus tips. Cover with mayonnaise and smooth the top.

Cut the egg white into slices and arrange a flower shape in the center. Decorate with fresh flowers if available for a different effect.

Salads and snacks

A chilled Ham Mold is ideal for a buffet party.

Ham Mold

1 lb cooked ham
1½ cups mushrooms
3 cups fine fresh white breadcrumbs
1 tbsp tomato paste
a little thick basic cheese sauce
2 egg yolks
mace
salt and pepper

To garnish
cooked peas
watercress
5–6 cucumber slices

Grind cooked ham and chop mushrooms finely. Mix together with the breadcrumbs and tomato paste and bind with the cheese sauce and egg yolks. Season to taste with a dash or two of mace and black pepper. Oil a 2½ cup ring mold and fill with mixture, pressing in well. Wrap mold in foil, place in a steamer, bring water to the boil and steam for about an hour. Top up the water in the steamer pan if necessary. Remove mold carefully from steamer, unwrap foil and turn out mold on to a serving dish.

When cool, fill the center with a handful of cooked peas, or watercress, to garnish. Surround with half slices of cucumber.

For a luxury touch, add ⅛ cup of chopped pistachio nuts to the mixture.

Rémoulade of Celery

4 stalks of celery
about ¼ cup light cream
paprika to garnish

For sauce
1¼ cups basic mayonnaise
juice of ½ lemon or 2 tbsp tarragon vinegar
1 tbsp white wine vinegar (optional)
1 tbsp Dijon mustard
1 tbsp chopped capers
1 tsp chopped fresh tarragon or
  ½ tsp dried tarragon
salt and pepper

Wash and cut celery into julienne (matchstick) strips.

Stir celery into the light cream and sprinkle with paprika. In another bowl, mix together mayonnaise, lemon juice or tarragon vinegar, extra vinegar (if necessary), mustard, chopped capers and tarragon. Season with salt and pepper. (The sauce should taste quite strongly of vinegar and mustard.) Serve with the prepared celery.

This rémoulade sauce is also good served with chopped celeriac, or hard-cooked eggs. A little sour cream may be added and beaten in if a lighter sauce is required.

Savory Rice Salad

1 lb long grain rice
1 cup diced leftover cooked
    white meat or poultry
pitted green olives
pitted black olives
1 cup canned pimientos
1¼ cups mushrooms
oil for frying
¼ lb peas
2–3 tomatoes
grated rind of 1 orange
⅔ cup basic French dressing

To garnish
watercress

Cook and drain rice. Spread out on a foil-covered cookie sheet to cool. Slice olives, cut pimientos into tiny dice. Slice mushrooms and shallow fry in a little oil. Cook peas; chop tomatoes into small pieces.

Mix together all the prepared ingredients in a salad bowl and toss in French dressing flavored with grated orange rind. Garnish with sprigs of watercress.

If wished, a generous ⅓ cup of basic mayonnaise may also be used, in addition to the French dressing, to bind and flavor salad.

Golden Egg Snacks

1 egg
½ unsliced white loaf
2 small slices cooked ham, beef
    or luncheon meat
1 tbsp butter or margarine
2 level tbsp cold mashed potatoes
watercress to garnish
salt and pepper

Separate the egg. Cut two rounds of bread approximately ½ inch thick and 2–3 inches in diameter, with a plain cookie cutter. Cut two similar slices from the cooked meat. Lightly butter the bread rounds and place the meat on top. In a bowl, mix the egg yolk with the mashed potato, season to taste and spread carefully over the meat. Whip egg white until it holds its shape well and pile on to each snack.

Heat the oil in a deep fat pan until a cube of bread rises to the surface, bubbles and browns in 20 seconds. Using a slotted spoon, carefully lower the snacks one at a time into the hot fat, and baste oil over the whipped egg white until golden brown. Drain and serve immediately garnished with the watercress. Add a side salad for a more substantial snack.

Egg Salad Nests

4 eggs
4 medium carrots
¼ of a medium white or green cabbage
4–6 medium tomatoes
basic lemon mayonnaise

Hardcook the eggs; peel and grate carrots. Shred cabbage into thin strips; scald and skin tomatoes. Make up the mayonnaise.

Slice the eggs crosswise and arrange each on the center of an individual serving dish. Arrange a ring of grated carrot around each egg and surround this carrot ring with a ring of shredded cabbage. Cut tomatoes into slices and discard seeds. Arrange tomato slices around the edge of the cabbage and, if liked, pipe rosettes of lemon mayonnaise between each slice of tomato. Hand extra mayonnaise separately.

Golden Egg Snacks.

Salads and snacks

Spanish Eggs are baked eggs on a delicious meat and vegetable mixture.

Spanish Eggs

5 eggs
¼ cup cooked pork
¼ cup cooked ham
1 medium onion
4–5 small tomatoes
¼ cup butter or margarine
¼ cup flour
½ cup strong stock
chopped parsley to garnish
salt and pepper

Set the oven at 350°F.

Finely dice pork and ham. Peel and grate onion. Skin, and chop the tomatoes.

Melt the butter or margarine in a pan and add the pork, the ham and the onion. Cook for a few minutes until the onion is transparent. Add flour and stir until blended. Add chopped tomatoes and the stock, little by little. Allow to simmer over gentle heat until mixture is thick and smooth. Season to taste, transfer mixture to a shallow ovenproof dish and break the eggs, one by one, over the mixture.

Cook in the oven until eggs are set – about 20–30 minutes. Garnish with chopped parsley to serve.

Beetroot and Onion Salad

1 large cooked beetroot or 4 small ones
1 tbsp wine vinegar
1 large onion or 2 medium ones
⅔ cup strong stock

Rub skin off the beetroot, if not already peeled. Cut into thin sticks, each about 1½ inches long and put into a bowl with the wine vinegar. Peel onion and cut into thin rings. Add to beetroot and chill. When ready to serve, bring the stock to the boil. Pour over beetroot and onions and serve.

Use a bunch of chopped scallions instead of the larger onions if preferred.

For a quick and easy snack, try Italian Eggs.

Italian Eggs

1 lb fresh spinach
a dash of nutmeg
2 tbsp butter or margarine
⅛ cup grated Parmesan cheese
1–2 tbsp light cream
5 eggs
½ cup milk
1 tbsp wine vinegar (optional)
10 bread croûtes, cut into triangles, or
    10 squares of buttered toast
salt and pepper

Remove stalks from spinach, wash leaves well and place in a pan over low heat. Cook until the spinach is tender, stirring to prevent it sticking to the pan. It should take about 7–10 minutes. Rub cooked spinach through a sieve to obtain a purée or use a blender taking care not to over-blend the spinach. Season with salt and pepper, and nutmeg, the butter or margarine, and the cheese. Add a little cream or milk, if necessary, and spread spinach over a shallow, ovenproof dish. Keep hot.

Make the bread croûtes by dipping crustless slices of bread in a mixture of one beaten egg and the ½ cup of milk. Fry in a little hot oil until brown and crisp. Place round the cooked spinach and keep hot.

Poach the four remaining eggs. If using a pan of water, add 1 tablespoon of wine vinegar to help stop the egg white spreading all over the pan. Make sure the water is moving gently, not bubbling fiercely, and slide eggs carefully into pan. Cook until just set.

Drain well, place on spinach, season and serve hot.

Salads and snacks

Quick Pizza Napolitana for an Italian flavor.

Quick Pizza Napolitana

bread dough or basic puff pastry
  made from 1½ cups flour
½–¾ cup grated Emmenthaler or
  Mozzarella cheese
¾ cup pitted green and black olives
8 anchovy fillets
4 medium tomatoes
pinch of dried mixed herbs or dried basil
a little cooking oil
freshly ground black pepper

Set the oven at 400°F.

If using bread dough, make as usual and allow to prove twice. To save time, you can prove once, and then continue to make the pizza. Leave to rise in a warm place for 10–15 minutes before baking.

Roll out dough or puff pastry into a circle, about ¼ inch thick. Place on an oiled cookie sheet.

Slice anchovy fillets in half and soak in a little milk, if liked, to remove excess salt. Skin and slice the tomatoes. Sprinkle the circle of dough or pastry with grated cheese, dot surface with olives. Drain and arrange anchovy fillets in between the olives; scatter the sliced tomatoes over the surface. Add a generous pinch or two of dried mixed herbs, or basil, and sprinkle surface with drops of cooking oil. Sprinkle with black pepper.

Bake in the preset oven until dough or pastry is golden brown and cooked – about 20–30 minutes.

A bread mix may be used for this pizza. In which case, bake base before filling, then slide pizza under broiler to cook through the topping, until cheese bubbles.

Provençal Onion Flan

basic shortcrust pastry made from 1½ cups
  flour
1½ lb onions
2 cloves of garlic
16–20 anchovy fillets
3 tbsp oil
3 tbsp butter or margarine
32 pitted black olives

Set the oven at 375°F.

Make up pastry. Peel and slice onions into very thin rings. Peel and chop garlic finely. Slice anchovy fillets into very thin strips. Soak in a little milk.

Roll out pastry very thinly and line into a shallow 10 inch flan ring placed on a greased cookie sheet. Prick the base with a fork and chill. Heat butter and oil in a frypan and fry onion rings with garlic over a low heat until transparent, but not brown. Turn into pastry case. Make a lattice pattern of anchovy strips and olives.

Bake for about 30–35 minutes.

A savory such as Provençal Onion Flan is perfect for a picnic or light snack.

Index

Index